7 Commitments
of a Forerunner

by Mike Bickle
with Brian Kim

IHOP.org
MikeBickle.org

7 Commitments of a Forerunner
by Mike Bickle with Brian Kim

Published by Forerunner Publishing
International House of Prayer
3535 E. Red Bridge Road
Kansas City, MO 64137
forerunnerpublishing@ihop.org
IHOP.org
MikeBickle.org

Printed in the United States of America

ISBN: 978-0-9823262-7-5

Cover design by Isaac Reichenbach

Table of Contents

CHAPTER 1

The Need of this Hour

We stand at a critical juncture in our nation's history. The Holy Spirit is visiting His people with power. At the same time, the powers of darkness are raging against the moral fabric of our nation. As the light becomes brighter, the darkness grows darker. In this strategic hour of history, the Spirit is speaking clearly to the Church, and many are responding to what He is saying. Will you be one of those who respond in a wholehearted way? Will you set your heart to say, "Yes, Lord," and follow through regardless of the cost?

Just a brief glance at today's headlines reveals the urgency of the hour. All around the earth, nations convulse under the threat of natural disasters, lawlessness, wars, and rumors of wars (Mt. 24:4-12). Entire nations in the West tremble at the menace of radical Islam and seek to acquiesce to its demands, in the hope of "peaceful" coexistence, even as Islam marches towards global domination. Beyond the haunting specter of radical Islam, the prevailing sentiment worldwide is becoming one of fear, unbelief, and mistrust as the earth shudders under the weight of man's sinful ways (Isa. 24:5-6).

The crisis only deepens as we examine what is going on beneath the façade of the fading American dream, as the corruption of sin digs its claws deeper and deeper into the hearts and minds of many. The serpentine stranglehold of abortion continues to squeeze the life out of over 4,000 wombs daily. The sanctity of marriage has come under siege like at no other time, threatening to destroy the moral foundations of our nation. Entire school systems are giving way to this darkness. The number of women and children being trafficked into the dark underbelly of the sex industry is growing at an alarming rate. Sexual immorality, both heterosexual and homosexual, is reaching epic heights of depravity in our nation. With easy access to pornography via the Internet and the hyper-sexualization of our culture promoted by MTV and Hollywood, a generation has been seduced into a dark cesspool that pollutes both body and soul. The list could go on and on.

There is also a growing crisis that is emerging in many churches across America. A new wave of confusion is subtly yet systematically seducing many young adults into deception. Sincere young people whose hearts were once ablaze for Jesus are being allured into compromise on foundational biblical truths and practices. The true danger of this new kind of "Christianity" is obscured by the works of compassion and justice that its followers are engaged in. However, they fail to recognize that no amount of increased ministry activity can "balance out" the profound spiritual and scriptural compromises that they are embracing. Yes, they are doing more and more in the name of justice and compassion, but less and less in the name of Jesus. In the name of tolerance, they are settling for a humanistic and "politically correct" theology that trivializes the glory of Jesus. Many young adult ministries are falling prey to this deception as they seek a form of relevance that dulls the razor's edge of truth for the sake of man's approval. It is not enough to mention Jesus' name if they deny foundational truths about Him. Our theology and spirituality, as well as our works of compassion and justice, must flow from *deep allegiance to Jesus and His Word.*

In the past few years, a new movement known as the "Emergent Church" has surfaced in the West, masquerading as a new and improved version of Christianity. The ideas propagated by the Emergent Church have captured the imagination of a multitude of young adults and are leading them down a dangerous and risky path to deception and heresy.

This movement purposefully refuses to define most of its beliefs and leaders. This in no way obscures the reality that the primary voices that shape their "conversation" are having a destructive influence on many young believers who, though undoubtedly sincere, lack discernment in basic biblical truths. We recognize that there are some leaders in their midst who are seeking to hold to historic evangelical truths. However, the overall "sound" emerging from this undefined movement significantly undermines essential biblical truths. God is raising up clear voices from many different parts of the Body of Christ who are unmasking the dangerous seductions of the Emergent Church as they expose its unorthodox and heretical beliefs.

Our nation has never stood on such a precarious footing as today. The onslaught of spiritual darkness is increasing in our classrooms, boardrooms, courtrooms, and bedrooms. Confusion is pouring forth from many pulpits, as well as from the halls of Washington. It is time for the uncompromising voice of forerunners to speak clearly in the midst of so much confusion. Yes, it is time to draw a line in the sand and to take a bold stand for truth.

We live in a very significant hour of history. I believe we are in the time described in the Scripture as the "beginning of sorrows," or "the beginning of birth pains," that precedes the Great Tribulation (Mt. 24:4-8, 21). The Bible tells us that during the

Great Tribulation, sin will become fully *ripe* with unprecedented and unimaginable levels of murder, witchcraft, sexual immorality, and theft manifesting throughout the earth (Rev. 9:21; 14:18).

During that time, a ruler more ruthless and evil than the world has ever encountered will emerge from the stage of world politics after consolidating worldwide power (Dan. 7; 2 Thes. 2; Rev. 13) This man, commonly known as the Antichrist, will wage war against the people of God, causing the greatest persecution and oppression of the Church in history (Dan. 7:25; Rev. 13:7). Consequently, the earth will be stained with the blood of the martyrs (Rev. 6:9; 16:6; 17:6). Equally challenging to these unprecedented events will be the release of God's judgments, which will be poured out upon the Antichrist and his reprobate empire. God will judge these reprobate people for their oppression of His own people. Jesus, our great deliverer, will not be silent at this time, but will release His judgments to remove all that hinders love (Lk. 18:7-8; Rev. 19:2).

The Scriptures are clear that many will fall away and depart from the faith in the midst of the crisis, as fear, offense, and deception abound (Mt. 24:9-13; Lk. 21:26; 2 Thes. 2:3; 1 Tim. 4:1-2; 2 Tim. 3:1-7; 4:3-5; 2 Pet. 2:1-3). A theological crisis across the nations will perplex many who will be unable to discern between truth and deception (1 Tim. 4:1-3). Today's hollow programs, prayerlessness, and preaching of a false gospel of cheap grace in many places will not prepare believers for the coming revival of glory or the encroaching storm of darkness. In the midst of this, many will be confused and even offended by the idea that God will release powerful judgments against the Antichrist and his reprobate followers. There will be a great need for the clear prophetic voices of forerunners to speak into the confusion.

It is always darkest before the dawn, and so our hearts remain full of faith. We know that a "Great Awakening" is soon to sweep across our nations. Though many see no hope, no solution to the coming crisis, we look with confidence to God's promises to pour out His Spirit on all flesh in the last days (Acts 2:17-21), when all nations will receive the witness of the kingdom with power (Mt. 24:14; Rev. 7:9). What a privilege to live in this awesome hour of history!

Forerunners Announce the Second Coming of Jesus

End-time forerunners announce the second coming of Jesus, as well as the great revival and pressures that are directly related to His return. In these days, God is beginning to prepare forerunners from many different streams in the Body of Christ worldwide. The forerunner message emphasizes Jesus' second coming, while proclaiming and manifesting the power of Jesus' first coming, as forerunners win the lost, heal the sick, help the poor, and walk in love and holiness.

What was fully accomplished at His first coming will be *fully manifest in all the nations* in the events related to His second coming. We will develop this more in the next chapter.

Forerunners Must Hear What the Spirit Is Saying

Forerunners must hear what the Spirit is saying to them in this hour and act on it. It is time for them to seek to live with a new depth of obedience and responsiveness to the Spirit. Even in this hour, the Lord is now calling some to embrace a season of rigorous preparation that will equip them to more effectively proclaim the forerunner message in the midst of the coming pressures.

End-time forerunners can find inspiration and instruction from New Testament forerunners like John the Baptist, the first apostles, and the seventy disciples, who all announced the first coming of Jesus to their generation (Mt. 10:5-8; Lk. 9:1-2; 10:1).

John the Baptist functioned as a forerunner by announcing the coming of Jesus, as well as the glory and pressures that would result from it in that generation (Lk. 3:3-9, 16-18).

The apostles functioned as forerunners in two ways. First, they announced the first coming of Jesus to the cities of Israel (Lk. 9:1-6). Second, they proclaimed the second coming of Jesus and the worldwide glory and pressures that would result in that generation (Acts 3:19-21; 2 Pet. 3; 1. 4-5; 2 Thes. 1-2; Rev. 6-19).

End-time forerunners will imitate the *message* of John the Baptist and the New Testament apostles by proclaiming the first coming of Jesus and the salvation accomplished by it, as well as proclaiming the second coming of Jesus and the unique dynamics created by events related to it.

Forerunners will imitate the *lifestyle* of John the Baptist and the New Testament apostles, who rejected the professional robes of religion for a lifestyle of radical obedience to Jesus and walking in the power of the Spirit. This will involve embracing a lifestyle that includes much prayer with fasting as they seek to go deep in the Word, while at the same time winning the lost, healing the sick, making disciples, church planting, and operating in the power of the Spirit to meet the needs of people.

As forerunners proclaim the Word and do the works of the kingdom, they glorify Jesus and deliver the oppressed; *by the very same activity,* they are being preparing to be used even more in the years ahead.

As the end-time revival approaches and storm clouds gather, the lifestyle of John the Baptist and the apostles will become increasingly relevant to this generation. They serve as an inspiration and as a model of forerunners who announce the Jesus' return.

This, then, begs the question: what kind of people were men like John the Baptist, Peter, and Paul? How did they live? They gave up all to follow Jesus, prayed and fasted much, diligently studied the Word, proclaimed Jesus' first and second comings, ministered in the power of the Spirit, and joyfully endured persecution.

Jesus' own testimony over John's life was that John was the "greatest man born of a woman" (Mt. 11:11). After Herod beheaded John for his uncompromising message, Jesus again testified about him, saying that "He [John the Baptist] was the burning and shining lamp, and you were willing for a time to rejoice in his light" (Jn. 5:35). John described himself as the "friend of the Bridegroom" whose joy was fulfilled because he heard the Bridegroom's voice (Jn. 3:29). With these accolades from the very lips of Jesus and John's own words as a guide, it is wise for this generation to pay attention to the radical dedication and message of John the Baptist.

We cannot view John's abandonment to God merely as an historical anomaly or the exception of a time long past, unattainable in the twenty-first century. Some seek to dismiss John as irrelevant for today because he was the final prophet of the old covenant. However, John was also the first follower of Jesus and the first evangelist who actually called people to follow Jesus. John was the first to disciple some of the very men who Jesus chose as His apostles (Jn. 1:35-42). He was a devoted follower of Jesus and was also an effective soul-winner and disciple-maker. We would do better to learn from John than to dismiss him.

Peter gave up all to follow Jesus (Mt. 19:27), prayed and fasted much (Mt. 9:15; Acts 6:4), proclaimed Jesus' first and second comings (Lk. 9:1-6; Acts 3:19-21; 2 Pet. 3), ministered in signs and wonders, and endured rejection and persecution (Acts 3:6-8; 4:1-12; 5:12-42).

Paul sacrificed many things to follow Jesus (Phil. 3:7-8), prayed and fasted often (Rom. 12:12; 2 Cor. 6:5; 11:27; 1 Thes. 3:10), diligently studied the Scripture (Gal. 1:11-17), and suffered much persecution (2 Cor. 11:23-29). He faithfully proclaimed the first and second coming of Jesus and the events related to it (1 Cor. 15:3-4; 1 Thes. 4-5; 2 Thes. 1-2).

Peter and Paul are models of dedication to Jesus and New Testament ministry. Neither can we see their abandonment to God as out of reach for the twenty-first-century believer. Rather, we must recognize that lives of John the Baptist, Peter, and Paul serve as a prophetic call to radical abandonment to Jesus and the purposes of God in our generation.

Jesus used John the Baptist's life and ministry to exemplify what it meant when He said, "The kingdom of heaven suffers violence, and the violent take it by force" (Mt. 11:12). Jesus was not referring in any way to physical violence, but to an interior spiritual "violence" characterized by radical obedience and love for God. Jesus aptly describes this sort of radical abandonment to God as spiritual "violence," because such radical obedience is disruptive to worldly pursuits and mindsets. It violently confronts our sinful desires, pride, and selfishness.

It violently reorders our priorities, including the way we pursue comfort, honor, and success; the way we spend our time, money, and energy; and the way we express our sexuality. Spiritual violence speaks of holy intensity in pursuing and loving God and people. This sort of spiritual violence is motivated by love and declares war on our sin, selfishness, and compromise. It refuses anything that may hinder love for God and people, seeking to be wholly dedicated to the kingdom of God.

Unfortunately, radical dedication is rarely found in the context of the Western church. It has been seen for causes far less impressive and worthy than the cause of Christ. Communists of previous generations displayed more zeal for their false causes than Western Christians do today for the truth and majesty of Jesus. Recognizing this, Billy Graham, at InterVarsity's 1957 Urbana conference, rebuked the Church in America for its lack of zeal for God, and went on to read the following excerpt from a letter written by a student who was writing to his girlfriend to break off their engagement after he had become a Communist:

> We Communists have a high casualty rate. We're the ones who get shot and hung and lynched and tarred and feathered and jailed and slandered, and ridiculed and fired from our jobs, and in every other way made as uncomfortable as possible. A certain percentage of us get killed or imprisoned. We live in virtual poverty. We turn back to the party every penny we make above what is absolutely necessary to keep us alive.

> We Communists don't have the time or the money for many movies, or concerts, or T-bone steaks, or decent homes and new cars. We've been described as fanatics. We are fanatics. Our lives are dominated by one great overshadowing factor: the struggle for world Communism.

> We Communists have a philosophy of life which no amount of money could buy. We have a cause to fight for, a definite purpose in life. We subordinate our petty personal selves into a great movement of humanity, and if our personal lives seem hard, or our egos appear to suffer through subordination to the party, then we are adequately

compensated by the thought that each of us in his small way is contributing to something new and true and better for mankind.

There is one thing in which I am dead earnest and that is the Communist cause. It is my life, my business, my religion, my hobby, my sweetheart, my wife and mistress, my bread and meat. I work at it in the daytime and dream of it at night. Its hold on me grows, not lessens as time goes on. Therefore I cannot carry on a friendship, a love affair, or even a conversation without relating to this force which both drives and guides my life. I evaluate people, books, ideas, and actions according to how they affect the Communist cause and by their attitude toward it. I've already been in jail because of my ideas and if necessary, I'm ready to go before a firing squad.

—Billy Graham, Urbana Conference 1957[1]

To be clear, such spiritual violence is not *required* to enter into the kingdom, but it is "suffered," which means it was *allowed*, or *permitted*, and even rewarded by God. God desires that we seek Him with spiritual violence and be utterly abandoned to Him. He is loved and honored when His people seek Him with a spiritual fervor, laying aside everything that gets in the way of obeying and loving Him with all of their heart. If we come with a willing heart, God will release transforming grace in the midst of our immaturity. Because of His grace, God *will* bring forth forerunners who will pursue Jesus like John the Baptist, Peter, and Paul. He has given His Spirit as a Helper. Thus, a lifestyle of

[1] www.urbana.org/articles/mission-commitment

dedication resembling John the Baptist and the apostles is available to anyone who refuses to settle for anything less.

Having considered the crisis that confronts our generation, we must identify the biblical lifestyle that will prepare us to be part of the corresponding solution. These seven commitments of a forerunner are merely a starting point in defining a few practical ways to walk out the forerunner lifestyle:

- *Pray Daily*: connecting with God while changing the world by releasing His power.

- *Fast Weekly*: positioning ourselves to receive more from God by fasting two days a week.

- *Do Justly*: being zealous for good works of compassion and justice that exalt Jesus as we impact the seven spheres of society.

- *Give Extravagantly*: experiencing the joy of financial power encounters as we sacrificially give money to the kingdom and support the prayer movement.

- *Live Holy*: living fascinated in the pleasure of loving God that overflows to loving people.

- *Lead Diligently*: taking initiative to minister to others and make disciples by regularly leading in outreaches, prayer meetings, and Bible studies.

- *Speak Boldly*: being a faithful witness of the truth with allegiance to Jesus' Word.

These seven commitments are not a comprehensive list covering the entire Christian life—they are a few practical, spiritual activities and disciplines that will serve as a launching pad to prepare us to walk out the forerunner ministry. The forerunner lifestyle is not reserved for the elite; it is available to anyone who is willing to heed the call to *decrease* so that Jesus might *increase* in and through their lives. However, we must take care, because a spirit of pride about our dedication will defile our spirit and hinder our spiritual growth.

Though these seven commitments are not complicated, they must be faithfully cultivated step by step, day by day, year after year. We must commit to keep them even when other opportunities present themselves that might cause us to lay the commitments aside. We cannot treat these commitments to a kingdom lifestyle as optional practices to live out only when they are convenient and when nothing else is going on. We are to see them as *sacred*, or very valuable and important to us, even when other desires and opportunities come our way. People who give themselves faithfully to these disciplines will certainly bear great fruit today in serving others, while at the same time preparing themselves to powerfully announce the coming of King Jesus and the events related to His return.

CHAPTER 2

Forerunners Proclaiming
the Coming of Jesus

In my opinion, we are in the early days of the generation in which Jesus will return. I believe that there are people alive today who will see the return of Jesus. It may be the 20-year-olds or it could be the 2-year-olds who see His return. I do not know. No one can know this with certainty. However, I do know that the Lord will raise up forerunners in the generation in which He returns. What is a forerunner? Forerunners proclaim the coming of the Lord and the events directly related to it. When we look at the first-century forerunners, it gives us insight into the life and role of forerunners in the end times. John the Baptist and the apostles were first-century forerunners; they went into various cities before Jesus in order to proclaim His coming.

> [Jesus] . . . sent messengers before His face. And as they went, they entered a village of the Samaritans, to prepare for Him.
>
> —Luke 9:52

The angel Gabriel alluded to Isaiah 40 when he described

John the Baptist as a forerunner who would prepare people to receive Jesus at His first coming (Lk. 1:11-19).

> It is he who will go as a *forerunner* before Him in the spirit and power of Elijah, to turn the hearts of the fathers back to the children, and the disobedient to the attitude of the righteous; so as to make ready a people prepared for the Lord.
> —Luke 1:17, NAS

> The voice of one crying in the wilderness: "Prepare the way of the LORD; make straight in the desert a highway for our God."
> —Isaiah 40:3

John the Baptist was a voice crying in the wilderness to prepare the way of the Lord (Jn. 1:23). These passages give us insight into the forerunner ministry as that of preparing people by announcing the coming of Christ. John was a prophet who also ministered as an evangelist, calling multitudes to come to Jesus. In other words, he announced the coming of Jesus while winning souls to the kingdom and making disciples by teaching them to pray, fast, and live righteously (Mt. 9:14; Lk. 3:3-18; 11:1).

Isaiah 62 describes forerunners in the generation in which the Lord returns: they will prepare people by building up the highway of the Lord and by lifting a banner message to the ends of the earth that God's salvation is surely coming. Forerunners proclaim the second coming of Jesus and give insight into the reward that He will bring with Him (Rev. 22:12).

> Prepare the way for the people; build up, build up the highway! Take out the stones, lift up a banner for the peoples! Indeed the LORD has

> proclaimed to the end of the world: "Say to the
> daughter of Zion, 'Surely your salvation is com-
> ing; behold, His reward is with Him, and His
> work before Him.'"
>
> —Isaiah 62:10-11

Just as the first-century forerunners proclaimed the first coming of Jesus ahead of time, so also the end-time forerunners will
proclaim the second coming of Jesus ahead of time. I believe
that even now, God is beginning to prepare forerunners from
many different streams in the Body of Christ worldwide. These
forerunners will function in many different ways and with different ministry callings. They include those called as evangelists,
pastors, teachers, prophets, media missionaries, artists, singers,
musicians, actors, writers, and those called to the marketplace.
Many will focus on making disciples by leading small groups
in their church, university, or work place. Moms and dads are
some of the most effective forerunners as they teach their children about the coming of Jesus and its implication. The forerunner ministry is not reserved for some elite group of people—it
is a calling available to any believer who is willing to announce
the coming of Jesus and the events related to it.

Forerunners Proclaim Both Comings of the Lord

Forerunners emphasize Jesus' second coming at the same
time as proclaiming the benefits of His first coming as they win
the lost, heal the sick, help the poor, and walk in love and holiness. To understand the fullness of Jesus' earthly ministry, we
must consider the two time frames that are related to His first
and second comings. The first time frame started years before
the cross and extends through church history. The second time
frame starts three and a half years before His second coming and

extends through the millennial kingdom. The second time frame is referred to as the Day of the Lord.

Jesus' earthly ministry in these two time frames is joined together in God's plan to accomplish the fullness of His purposes. There is a *dynamic continuity* between these two. We must not see them as separate realities but as the same glory of Jesus being manifest in two periods of time.

What was fully accomplished at Jesus' first coming will be *fully manifest in all the nations* in the events related to His second coming. At His first coming, He paid the price for our sin and sickness, defeated Satan, and released the power of the Spirit in and through His people so that they might live in victory over sin and make a dynamic impact on the nations in this age. At His second coming, He takes it all a step further by openly manifesting the *fullness* of His victory in *every* sphere of life. Imagine the power that He will exert when He raises every believer from the dead, casts Satan into prison, fully transforms every area of society in every nation, and removes the curse of sin from creation by restoring all things, including the animals, atmosphere, and agriculture. All of these activities are aspects of Jesus' earthly ministry as described in various end-time scriptures.

Some only focus on the benefits of Jesus' first coming as it relates to His salvation and power being manifest over the last 2,000 years of church history. Others focus on the benefits of Jesus' first coming as it relates to the events of His second coming. These two periods are joined together in God's greater purposes. What God has joined together, let no man separate. We must proclaim the whole counsel of God, which includes His saving power being manifest on earth in both time frames (Acts 5:20; 20:20, 27).

Forerunners Live in Two Time Frames

Forerunners live both in the *now* and in the *future*. They press into the kingdom in the now while also preparing for the unique dynamics that will occur just before Jesus returns. They see the significance of the years leading up to His return, at which time extreme and unique dynamics—both positive and negative—will be occurring. These will include the greatest outpouring of the Spirit and revival in history, one that will surpass the book of Acts. It will also include Satan's most intense rage against the human race and God's most severe judgments being poured out against the Antichrist's empire.

Noah is an example of a forerunner who lived in two time frames, seeking to live in the fullness of God's purposes in the now while preparing for the fullness of God's purpose in the future. He poured himself out in preaching to unbelievers while he was preparing an ark for a future storm that would not occur for many decades (Heb. 11:7; 2 Pet. 2:5).

We do not need to choose between *now* and *then*. It is our inheritance to walk in the fullness of what God intended for both time frames. End-time forerunners announce the second coming of Jesus while they win the lost, heal the sick, and make disciples.

Forerunners Prepare the Unprepared

Simply defined, the forerunner ministry announces the coming of the Lord and prepares the unprepared to receive the ministry of Jesus in the midst of the unique dynamics of the end times. Not all ministries feel called to emphasize the second coming of Jesus and the events related to it. However, those who do must prepare today by gaining deeper understanding of what the Scripture says about the end times.

How will forerunners *practically* prepare the unprepared? By informing them that Jesus is returning to the earth as the King of kings and by changing their *expectation and interpretation* of the unique events related to His coming. They will prepare people to respond rightly to Jesus by giving them understanding of His end-time plans so that they will be able to *agree* with what He is doing in that hour instead of *resisting* it.

If people lack understanding of what is happening in the end times, they will be far more vulnerable to yield to fear, offense, confusion, compromise, and deception. Their ignorance of what the Scripture says about the events occurring in that hour will cause them to make wrong decisions. As intense events unfold, many will lose their perspective and objectivity in seeing God's love and wisdom. People will need to see what is happening from a biblical perspective and understand the events as an expression of God's love and wisdom. Forerunners will bring this understanding of God's love to the context of the unique end-time events. Others will just be confused, without knowing what is right or wrong. Unbelievers will have a desperate need to understand what is happening (Mt. 24:37-39). Even some believers will struggle with offense at Jesus for what He is allowing to happen (Mt. 11:6). In contrast, those who do understand what is happening will be far more likely to grow in faith and love. By gaining understanding they will be able to discern the right things and, therefore, to resist the wrong ones. Forerunners proclaim from the Scripture what will happen before it occurs, including the end-time revival, judgment, deception, and persecution.

Forerunners Bring Understanding of the Judgment of God

The purpose of God's judgments against the Antichrist's empire is to remove all that hinders love; they are expressions of

His love. Those who misunderstand God's judgments will be offended and angry with Him. Forerunners will help people receive Jesus' love instead of being offended at Him. People must rightly interpret Jesus' judgments in order to trust His leadership so that they may mature in love for Him. Forerunners will bring right understanding about God's judgments. It is not enough to make known the *fact* that God's judgments are coming against the Antichrist's empire—we must give the *reason* for them. We are to give the *why* behind the *what*.

At the heart of God's judgment is Jesus, intervening to deliver the oppressed and to stop oppressors. Think of the implications of a God who would not intervene to stop oppressors. What would you think of a father who would not intervene to prevent a man kidnapping his children? God's judgments are an expression of His love for His children. Furthermore, in the midst of those very judgments, God offers mercy to the oppressors if they will only repent and receive it. Isaiah proclaimed that when God's judgments are in the earth, the inhabitants of the world learn righteousness (Isa. 26:9).

Praying against the Judgment of God in this Hour

In this hour, the saints are not to pray for judgment against ungodly nations. They are to cry out for God's mercy to triumph over judgment in the midst of ungodly nations. We pray for their salvation and deliverance. At this time, we do not pray to release God's judgment, but to stop it. The message of the Old Testament prophets was that God's people could stop the judgment of God through intercession. We see this message clearly throughout the entire book of Joel.

The only time when the saints are to pray for the release of judgment against the Antichrist's empire is in the final three and half years of this age. We must be clear that God's end-time judgments are focused on the Antichrist's reprobate empire. Reprobate people are so hardened in their hatred of God that they have no desire to ever repent. As Moses prayed for God to release His judgments against a reprobate Pharaoh in Exodus chapters 7 to 12, so the saints will pray for God to release judgment against the Antichrist's empire that seeks to oppress and kill the saints.

The greatest miracles of Jesus will be released through His Church during the final three and a half years of this age, when He releases signs and wonders against the Antichrist that are similar to those He released through Moses (Mic. 7:15). However, during the three and a half years before Jesus returns, we will pray for the judgments described in the book of Revelation to be released against the Antichrist and his empire, which will be comprised of reprobate peoples and nations. The reprobate in that hour will be far more hostile against Jesus as they oppress the saints. In that day, the prayers of *all* the saints from throughout history will be released against the Antichrist's empire (Rev. 8:3-5; Ps. 149:6-9).

Forerunners Prepare Themselves in the Word

Forerunners prepare themselves by going deep in God through studying the Scripture in the context of prayer with fasting, resisting temptation, enduring difficulties, ministering to people, and learning to operate in the gifts of the Spirit. The ministry we do today glorifies Jesus and helps people *while at the same time* preparing us for the future. The ministry we do today is an essential part of our preparation for future ministry.

Forerunners must grow in their understanding of the Scripture. There are over 150 chapters in the Bible that focus on Jesus' second coming and the end-time events that are associated with it. In comparison, the four gospels that give us a record of

Jesus' ministry at His first coming total 89 chapters. The gospels give us a record of Jesus' ministry related to His first coming when He *redeemed us* from our sins. The 150 chapters on the end times reveal His ministry and the events related to His second coming when He will openly manifest His *rule over all the nations.* Many of God's people neglect these 150 chapters without considering that they come from the *same Bible,* reveal the *same Jesus,* and manifest the *same power* of the Spirit as the four gospels. These 150 chapters focus on Jesus' end-time plan and the demonstration of His signs and wonders in totally removing wickedness from the earth and fully establishing His peace, righteousness, and love in all the nations.

Forerunners will take time to gain understanding of what the Scriptures say about the end times so that they may prophetically declare it to others (Isa. 62:10-12; Jer. 23:20; 30:24; Dan. 11:33-35; 12:9-10; Joel 2:28-29; Mal. 4:5-6; Mt. 17:11; Acts 2:17-21; Rev. 11:3-6; 13:18). Jeremiah prophesied that in the last days God would give His people a supernatural ability to perceive His loving purposes in sending His judgments: "In the latter days you will *understand it perfectly*" (Jer. 23:20). Jeremiah went on to prophesy that God's messengers would *consider,* or search out, the Word of God to gain understanding of God's heart behind His end-time judgments (Jer. 30:24).

Daniel prophesied that people who having understanding in the end times shall instruct many:

> Those of the *people who understand* shall instruct many . . . Some of *those of understanding* shall fall [martyrdom], to refine them, purify them, and make them white, until the time of the end; because it is still for the appointed time.
>
> —Daniel 11:33-35

God is raising up forerunners like John the Baptist who will be a voice with clarity, power, and boldness in the midst of much confusion. They will be a voice of things to come, not merely an echo (Jn. 1:23). Simply knowing a few Bible principles will not be enough; forerunners must grow in their understanding of the Scripture that they might be a clear prophetic voice in that hour.

Partnership with Jesus Now and Then

Some spend time preparing to engage in partnership with Jesus *now* with no thought of preparing for partnership with Him in the uniqueness of the end-time events. Their rationale is that we do not need to prepare because Jesus will just take care of things Himself at that time. There is a fundamental contradiction in this mindset. Though they correctly see Jesus as desiring partnership with His people today to change the world, they are wrong in thinking that He will not seek the same partnership in the years just before He returns. The good news is that Jesus wants full partnership with us now *and* then.

Jesus desires deep partnership with His Bride in every stage of His work in this age and the age to come, especially in the world-changing events that will occur just before He returns. He will not suddenly turn a cold shoulder to His Bride in that hour to take everything into His own hands, bypassing His joy in working through His people. As surely as He heals the sick and overcomes the oppressor through the prayers of the saints now, He will do the same then. Jesus longs for deep partnership with His people in every stage of His work in this age and the age to come.

We must be as intentional about preparing to partner with Jesus in the end times as we are in the now. The intensity of life at that time will require special preparation, especially in our understanding.

The End-time Hope for All the Nations

The return of Jesus is called the blessed hope: "The blessed hope and glorious appearing of our great God and Savior Jesus Christ" (Titus 2:13). He will come to rule all the nations and His judgments will remove all oppression and rebellion against God from the entire earth. All nations will live in the joy of God's manifest presence with unprecedented prosperity, righteousness, unity, and goodness. The earth will enjoy an open heaven greater than at any time in history. Even the hostility of certain animals toward humans will be removed (Rom. 8:19-23). The entire earth will be healed as the land, water, and atmosphere are fully cleansed. The conditions of the garden of Eden will eventually fill the entire earth (Isa. 35:1-8; 51:3; Ezek. 34:29; 36:35; 47:6-12).

We will experience great advancements of God's kingdom on the earth even before Jesus returns, but it will increase even more dramatically after His return. There is a dynamic continuity between our labors and victories before He returns and the victories that He will establish after He returns. It will all work together as one seamless plan. The devil will be thrown into prison, and all evil laws and leaders will be replaced by those that are righteous and good (Rev. 20:1-6). The earth will not end—Satan and the kingdom of darkness on earth will end. This is the greatest hope imaginable for our future and the generations to come. We are agents of change who confront evil now with the love and power of Jesus. There is no fear in love. The martyrs will overcome as they are victorious in love over Satan and all the ways of the Antichrist (Rev. 12:11; 15:2). We cry "Come, Lord Jesus," asking Him to come and fully establish the work the Church has been involved in for 2,000 years in preaching His kingdom (Rev. 11:15).

Jesus Commanded His People to Know the Generation

As I stated at the beginning of this chapter, my opinion is that we are in the early days of the generation in which Jesus will return. While no one can know the day or hour of His return, it is possible to know the *generation* of Jesus' return, by observing the biblical signs of the times. My opinions on this generation are based on *observation* of the biblical signs, not on personal *revelation* such as prophetic visions. We must insist that our faith be based on what the Bible says, not on personal revelations about the timing of His return.

Jesus commanded one generation of believers to know that His return was near. Of course, it was the generation that would be alive to "see all these things," or the signs that He prophesied in Matthew 24. They were to *know* that the end, or His return, was near. Some confuse not being able to know the day and hour (v. 36) with not being able to know the generation (v. 34).

> When you see all these things, know that it is near—at the doors! . . . This generation will by no means pass away till all these things take place . . . Of that day and hour no one knows.
>
> —Matthew 24:33-36

A generation in Scripture ranges anywhere from 40 to 100 years (Gen. 15:13-16; Num. 32:13; Ps. 90:10; Mt. 1:17; Acts 7:6). Moses spoke of Israel's captivity in Egypt as lasting 400 years or 4 generations (Gen. 15:13). Thus, a generation could refer to 100 years. The 14 generations from Abraham to David averaged about 70 years each (Mt. 1:17). We are called to know or recognize the generation in which the Lord returns. The point is that when we know it is drawing near, we can only look up and lift up our heads:

"There will be signs in the sun, in the moon . . . and on the earth distress of nations, with perplexity, the sea and the waves roaring; men's hearts failing them from fear . . . Now *when these things begin to happen,* look up and lift up your heads, *because your redemption draws near.*" Then He spoke to them a parable: "Look at the fig tree . . ."

—Luke 21:25-26, 28-29

Jesus pointed out that many living in the last generation would not know that they were in the last generation (Mt. 24:37-39). But believers *can* know the generation just as Noah did. It should not catch the righteous off guard (1 Thes. 5:1-6). Jesus rebuked those of His generation for not seeing the prophetic signs of the times they were living in (Lk. 19:42-44). Paul taught that the Church should know the *times and seasons* related to Jesus' second coming (1 Thes. 5:1-6). Jesus and Paul both emphasized that the signs of the times can be known (Mt. 24:32-34; Lk. 21:25-29; 1 Thes. 5:1-6; 2 Thes. 2:1-11).

Jesus connected the timing of His return to specific events and trends. There are sign events and sign trends predicted in Scripture that alert us to the timing of Jesus' return. As these trends accelerate at the *same time* on a *global level,* making headline news, we are to understand that we are in a unique season in history leading to Jesus' return. The light and darkness will both increase (Isa. 60:2; Mt. 13:30). Today, most of these trends are accelerating. For the *first* time in history, *most* of these trends and *some* of the necessary developments that will lead to the sign events are happening in an alarming measure, at the *same* time, and on a global basis.

The good news is that there is much biblical information about this because Jesus wants us to be prepared for His endtime purposes.

Sign events include the rebirth of the state of Israel in 1948. Israel becoming a nation was a necessary development for the abomination of desolation to occur. Positive trends indicating that we are close to the generation in which the Lord will return include Jesus' prophecy that "this gospel of the kingdom will be preached in all the world as a witness to all the nations, and then the end will come" (Mt. 24:14). The leading missionary organizations project from statistical data that the gospel will be presented to all 6,000 ethnic people groups among the 238 nations by 2015. Positive trends that serve as signs of the times also include the salvation of Israel, the global prayer and worship movement (Isa. 62:6-7), the people of God walking in their bridal identity (Rev. 22:17; Mt. 25:1–13), the outpouring of the spirit of prophecy (Acts 2:17), unparalleled understanding of end-time prophecy (Jer. 23:20; 30:24; Dan. 11:33; 12:10), and the global youth focus in the kingdom in which fathers turn their hearts to love and serve the younger generation (Mal. 4:5-6), including the fatherless (abortion, orphans, human trafficking).

Jesus prophesied *twelve negative trends* that bring distress to the nations and indicate the generation of His return (Mt. 24:4-14; Lk. 21:11, 25). Most of these trends are escalating at a speed that poses a threat to the stability and peace of the nations. Many negative sign trends are recorded in Matthew 24, including deception and false prophets (vv. 4-5, 11, 24), ethnic conflict (v. 7), economic warfare (v. 7), famines, pestilences, and earthquakes (v. 8), hatred of believers (v. 9), relational breakdown in society (v. 10), and lawlessness, causing love to grow cold (v. 12). Further negative sign trends are recorded in Luke 21: fearful sights and signs in the sky (v. 11), and disturbances in the sea (v. 25). These trends have always existed in society, but in the end times they will have a distinct intensity that will make global headline news. God has a message to a generation in them; they are pro-phetic signs that are meant to give believers confidence that the Lord is near. Other trends include the harlot Babylon worldwide religion (Rev. 17:2-6), the falling away from the faith (Mt. 24:9-13; 2 Thes. 2:3; 1 Tim. 4:1-2; 2 Tim. 3:1-7; 4:3-5), persecution against believers and lawlessness abounding (Mt. 24:12; Rev. 14:18), human trafficking (Rev. 18:13; Joel 3:3), pornography, and scoffers and mockers against the emphasis of preparing for the Lord's return (2 Pet. 3:3-4).

In the next chapters we will consider each of the seven com-mitments of the sacred charge that together help us to prepare for and live out the biblical lifestyle of a forerunner. With John the Baptist, we say, "He must increase, but I must decrease" (Jn. 3:30).

CHAPTER 3
Pray Daily
Connecting with God while Changing the World

Our commitment to pray daily is expressed in three main ways, by cultivating intimacy with God, interceding for revival, and praying for the sick to be healed. We grow in intimacy with God best by pray-reading the Scripture and praying through a prayer list on a regular basis. Included in praying over the Scripture is a call to read the book of Revelation once a week. Many who desire to be forerunners are unfamiliar with this amazing book that is so relevant for the future.

Through prayer we can fellowship with God. Prayer is also the primary vehicle by which we can partner with God to shape history and bring healing to others. We are calling forerunners to commit to at least two hours of prayer a day in any of these three expressions.

We all long to encounter God, to do the works of the kingdom, and to change the world. We are destined to release God's love and power to others, as we heal the sick, participate in revival, and impact society. We are to cultivate a prayer culture in our lives and ministries that manifests the supernatural power of the

Spirit. I sometimes refer to intimacy and intercession as prayer "with my eyes closed," and healing and prophecy as prayer "with my eyes open." We set our heart to pray daily, sometimes with our eyes closed and sometime with our eyes open.

Most Christians recognize early on in their spiritual journey that prayer is an essential element for anyone pursuing the fullest life in God. Accordingly, they eagerly desire to cultivate a lifestyle of prayer in its various expressions. Yet, even recognizing how necessary prayer is, few remain consistent in it. Instead, they resign themselves to believing it will always be boring and dull. Therefore, many live without a vibrant connection to Jesus.

A consistent prayer life is not only foundational, but essential to the forerunner ministry—only through a lifestyle of prayer can we receive the fullness of what God has for us.

Prayer, or connection with God, is one of the primary ways that we express our love and devotion to Him. Jesus instructed us, "He who *abides in Me*, and I in Him, bears much fruit; for *without Me you can do nothing*" (Jn. 15:5). Prayer is a place of connectedness with God that equips us to walk out the first great commandment in first place in our lives, knowing that it will overflow in love towards others, so that we may also walk out the second commandment (Mt. 22:37–39).

Intimacy with God

We grow in intimacy with God when we come to understand that we are His beloved, by encountering God as our Father and Jesus as our Bridegroom King.

Prayer is much more than a spiritual discipline to be performed, or the means by which we find our way out of difficult circumstances. Prayer was never meant to be duty-based or merely results-oriented. Rather, it is the place of encounter with God where our spirit is energized as we grow in love with Him. Truly, prayer is the wellspring of life and the very pathway into union with God. Just as our body cannot live without water, so our heart cannot live without connectedness to God through prayer. As we dialogue with Him in prayer, He reveals glimpses of His personality, giving us revelation of His thoughts and feelings toward us. This is a necessary foundation for all who wish to grow in intimacy with God.

Our God Is a Tender Father and Passionate Bridegroom

Our journey to a life of prayer must have a right foundation, which is established by cultivating a right view of God. Without this, our prayer lives will not be sustained. Many have the all-too-common, wrong view of God that portrays Him as an angry taskmaster forcing us to endure conversation with Him to prove our devotion to Him, or as a stoic God who is uninterested in our lives. As we perceive God as the tender Father and Jesus as the passionate Bridegroom, we will be energized in our spirit to continue to seek Him with all our heart and strength. Having the right view of God will dramatically help us to nurture our prayer lives.

Encountering the father heart of God is foundational to growing in prayer. Jesus prayed for us that we might know that the Father loves us as the Father loves His Son, Jesus (Jn. 17:23). *The revelation that the Father loves us as He loves Jesus is a profound statement of our great value and worth to Him.* Additionally, Paul tells us that we have "received the Spirit of adoption by whom we cry out, 'Abba, Father'" (Rom. 8:15). In Hebrew, *abba* is a term of endearment for a father, much like *papa* in our culture, which maintains respect, but is also affectionate and intimate. The revelation of God as *Abba* and the knowledge of our identity as adopted children empower us to endure difficulties and reject Satan's accusations that we are hopeless failures, while emboldening us in the truth that we truly have access to the Father's heart. We will remain unsettled until we come to the assurance that we are enjoyed by God the Father, *even in our weakness*. This truth, that *Abba God* enjoys us even in our weakness, is a stabilizing anchor that buoys our prayer lives. As sons and daughters of God, we are able to approach God's throne as heirs of His power, without shame or hesitation.

In tandem with the revelation of the father heart of God, understanding Jesus as our Bridegroom and ourselves as His cherished Bride is a powerful reality that equips us to possess a vibrant prayer life (Eph. 5:29-32). Scripture teaches that the Church will increasingly identify herself as the *Bride* who calls Jesus the Bridegroom to return to earth (Rev. 22:17). The end-time prayer movement will consist of the Church established in her bridal identity. As the Bride of Christ, we are in a privileged position to experience God's heart and affection by knowing that He cherishes us as a bridegroom cherishes his bride (Isa. 62:4-5).

This message of the Bridegroom identity of Jesus includes the revelation of His emotions that He feels for us. In simple terms, we understand Jesus, the Bridegroom, not as mostly mad or sad when He thinks about us, but as One whose heart is full of gladness and fiery affections for His people. Jesus is revealed as being filled with tender mercy, gentleness, and patience as He deals with us in our weakness. This view of God serves as a powerful motivation to pray and seek nearness and communion with God.

In November 1995, I had a prophetic dream that highlighted this biblical truth. In the dream, the Lord spoke audibly to me as I stood on the stage in a large auditorium. He said, "Call the people *Hephzibah*." The Lord continued to instruct me in this dream: "Tell the people that I delight in them and rejoice over them like a bridegroom rejoices over a bride." In the dream, as soon as I called His people "*Hephzibah*" the power of God touched them. I woke up from the dream and turned to Isaiah 62:4, which says, "You shall be called Hephzibah." In Hebrew, *Hephzibah* means "the delight of the Lord." The Lord is raising up a multitude of men and women—singers, preachers, writers, and intercessors—all over the world, who will proclaim that God delights in His people. It will be normal for God's people to grow confident in His affections for them.

How we view God will determine how we approach Him in prayer. If we view Him as aloof or angry, we will not want to pray very much. When we see Him as a tender Father and passionate Bridegroom who desires for us to come to Him, then we will pray much more.

Praying Daily to Grow in Intimacy with God

The most substantial way in which we can bolster our prayer lives is by feeding on the Word of God. This includes engaging in an active conversation with God while we read His Word, which is very beneficial to growing in intimacy with God. Many are in the spiritual intensive care unit with a sick heart and a diminished spiritual appetite due to a lack of taking in the Word of God.

Praying the Word back to God is much different from Bible study. While I am a serious advocate of Bible study, it cannot be mostly about the accumulation of more information and facts. Instead, Bible study *must* lead to dialogue with God. Jesus rebuked the Pharisees, saying, "You search the Scriptures, for in them you think you have eternal life; and these are they which testify of Me. *But you are not willing to come to Me that you may have life*" (Jn. 5:39-40). In other words, Jesus is saying that

Bible information, by itself, cannot give us life. We must understand that the Bible testifies of Jesus not for the sake of our fact
collection, but *so we will come to Him and dialogue with Him* in
prayer, in order for our hearts to expand in love for Him.

Again, Bible study is important. Study alone, however, is not
enough, for it fails to bring the presence of God to our hearts.
The Bible was meant to be the conversational material that we
bring to God. For example, when we read a passage in the Bible
that tells us of God's love or mercy, we cannot just underline
the passage and move on. It is not enough to just think about the
passage or tell others about it. On the contrary, we *must* turn the
words of the Bible into an active dialogue with Him.

Practically speaking, if I am reading a passage such as Psalm
51:1, where David prayed, "Have mercy upon me, O God, according to your lovingkindness; according to the multitude of
Your tender mercies," first, *I thank God*, saying, "Thank you,
God, that You promise to have mercy on me." Next, *I ask Him
for more revelation.* I would pray something like, "Reveal Your
mercy more and more to me" and so on. Likewise, if I read a
passage like Matthew 22:39 that says, "You shall love your
neighbor as yourself," I first commit myself to obey it, then I
ask Jesus for help. I pray, "Lord, I set my heart to love people."
Then I ask the Holy Spirit to help me to love my neighbor well.
As I read through the Word, I pause to pray these short phrases
to God. Praying the Word helps me to enjoy my times of prayer
as He releases more and more of His presence in response to my
praying His Word.

Praying Daily for Justice and Revival

Prayer involves more than intimacy with God; it is also used
dynamically by God to release His justice. Intercession involves

speaking God's Word back to Him concerning a person, city, or nation. Intercession occurs when we pray for the release of God's power and blessing on others. Intercession is God's means of establishing His kingdom. It affects the spiritual atmosphere of any region we pray for. Justice goes forth most effectively in the context of night and day prayer. Scripture says, "Now shall not God bring about *justice* for His elect, who *cry out to Him day and night* . . .? I tell you that He will bring about *justice* for them quickly" (Lk. 18:7-8, NAS). When the believers of a city connect to God through prayer and in unity with one another, God has promised to release His justice upon the earth. Jesus emphasized the absolute necessity of continual *intercession* that causes justice to go forth. We are to intercede until we see the full release of God's purpose.

The act of speaking the Word of God back to God not only promotes intimacy between us and God, but is also the very means by which God releases His justice upon the earth. Speaking forth the Word of God back to God is the catalyst for releasing His power. The Father has chosen to govern the earth in partnership with His people through intercession. Our speaking His word back to Him in prayer is one of God's primary ways of bringing about change upon the earth.

One of the most fascinating aspects of intercession is that Jesus lives forever to make intercession (Heb. 7:25). We know that Jesus often prayed to the Father while He was on earth. Yet even now, after the resurrection and glorification of Christ, He intercedes, or speaks the Father's will back to Him in prayer to release God's power on earth. Jesus is fully God, yet He continues to release the Father's power by intercession. He will rule forever by releasing the Father's will through intercession (Ps. 2:9; Heb. 7:25).

Intercession is so simple. It involves speaking God's Word back to God. It is accessible to every believer. We can all release God's power or justice simply by speaking the words of God back to God in prayer. Although He does not need us, He takes joy in His people reigning with Him through intercession.

In Genesis 1, when God created the heavens and the earth, He ordained that Jesus speak forth the plans of His heart to release the power of the Spirit. The Father had many plans in His heart for the earth, and the Spirit was present in power, yet it remained dark, formless, and void until the Son spoke the word to release the Spirit's power. Jesus was functioning in a form of intercession throughout the first chapter of Genesis.

Today, God requires our intercession to release the fullness of His power and justice on earth. As we speak, or pray, God's will back to God, the Spirit releases it on the earth. If we do not speak out God's Word, then the power of the Spirit will not be released in the same measure. God requires holy, persevering, believing prayer to release the fullness of what is in His heart. The fullness of God's justice will only be released in the context of night and day intercession. God longs to release justice through the saints to impact the seven spheres of society—family; education; government (politics, law, and military); economy (business, science, and technology); arts (entertainment and sports); media; and religion.

When we pray, we confront and even displace the demonic forces behind injustice. Paul tells us, "We do not wrestle against flesh and blood, but against principalities, against powers, against the rulers of the darkness of this age, against spiritual hosts of wickedness in the heavenly places" (Eph. 6:12).

Significant dimensions of injustice on the earth are empowered demonically, and humanitarian work in itself cannot break the powers instituting injustice. Works of justice and humanitarian efforts are not sufficient in fighting the battle against injustice. Works of justice and intercession are deeply connected as one reality before God. As we give practical care to those facing injustice upon the earth, we must intercede for power to shift the powers in the spiritual atmosphere. Intercession and works of justice work together. Jesus did not simply give those who were sick kind words, nor did He merely pay for their medical bills; He drove out the demons that were causing their sickness. Likewise, it is not enough for us to comfort the sick or just feed the hungry without confronting the demonic influences that perpetuate injustice and cause sickness and poverty.

Prayer is a primary way in which we can partner with God to shape history and bring healing to others. Paul exhorts us: "In everything, by prayer and supplication, with thanksgiving, let your requests be made known to God" (Phil. 4:6). A powerful, foundational principle of the kingdom of God is that we ask Him for everything, both the giving of good things along with deliverance from negative things.

Wondrously, *God actually responds to our asking*. This reality, perceived rightly, helps us to recognize that prayer is not only a fierce struggle, but a glorious privilege.

Through Jesus' mediating work on the cross, we have been given access to stand before the Father in confidence, trusting that He hears our cry and is moved by the sound of our voice. In prayer we can partner with Jesus to shape the destinies of cities as well as our families and friends.

Praying Daily for the Sick and Oppressed

Scripture commands us to pray for the sick and oppressed (Mt. 10:8; Mk. 16:17; Jas. 5:14-15). It is a commandment, not an option. If we think it is optional, then we can put it off until the future instead of engaging in the prayer of faith today. The Lord wants us to operate in the supernatural ministry of the Spirit as a lifestyle.

The rule of the kingdom is that God's power is released when His people declare or give testimony to His Word. In other words, the Holy Spirit releases more power as God's people speak His Word over those in need. If you are in a room of sick people and no one prays for them, then usually none of them will be healed. If someone simply prays over the sick in faith then healings will begin to occur. The Lord releases His Spirit following a declaration or a testimony of the Word. That is why we have to take time to pray the Word over people. The Spirit will move much more if we will simply speak the Word over people. He is waiting on us. He will heal more people if we will pray over them. Set your heart to pray for someone who is sick every day for the rest of your life, whether at home, on campus, at the mall, at work, or during vacation. We can do the works of the kingdom every day.

Today, we are to pray for the sick as a lifestyle, whether in the ministry line at a church service, at the shopping mall, in our dorm room, in our home, in the coffee shop, or wherever we may be. Praying for the sick and prophesying is to be a part of our everyday life. We can pray with confidence that the Spirit is listening and will move in power.

The Tension in the Kingdom

The tension many experience is in operating in faith now with gratitude while earnestly seeking God for a historic breakthrough of the fullness of the Spirit. We can operate in the power of God now while we continue to pray for a historic breakthrough that surpasses the book of Acts.

Some who pray for a historic breakthrough lose sight of ministering in the power of God in the now. And some who regularly minister to people now lose sight of contending in intercession for a historic breakthrough of the Spirit. In other words, they pour out all of their energy in the now and do not have faith or energy to contend for a breakthrough in the future, or vice versa.

We can have the fullness of what God has ordained for us now as well as seeking the fullness of what He has planned for the future. We can see blind eyes open now before the great end-time revival breaks out. We can win thousands of people to Jesus today, even before great multitudes get saved in our cities in the end-time revival. We can operate in both a present mode and a future mode.

We are to take hold of God's power today as well as contending for the fullness for tomorrow. In other words, we can have a "present-tense relationship" with Jesus while contending for a historic breakthrough of the Spirit's power. We can have both. We do not have to choose one or the other. Sadly, some who intercede for a breakthrough to heal the sick in the future do not pray to heal the sick today! I know some faithful intercessors who rarely pray for the sick. They live only in a "waiting mode" for a future breakthrough, instead of a "go mode" to see miracles today. The Lord wants us to operate in both modes.

Prayer that Protects Us from Burnout

Prayer positions us to be energized to love God and to love people, serving as a buffer against spiritual burnout. Remaining connected to Jesus at the heart level is the lifeline that enables us to sustain ministry in healing the sick and doing works of justice and compassion for decades. Without prayer, spiritual burnout is inevitable after a few years of active service. Intimacy with

Jesus is the only way to sustain the ability to serve others over the decades, so that we may more fully release justice on earth. Prayer that leads to intimacy with God protects our spirit from burnout while we minister long hours to people.

We have enough time to go deep in God and to reach out to people. We do not have to give up our personal prayer time to make time to minister to people. We can do both. We can "steal" more time for the kingdom from the time we spend on recreation and entertainment.

Practical Issues in Developing a Consistent Prayer Life

Part of the reason that too few people engage in prayer to grow in communion and intimacy with God is due to the fact that our culture has grown increasingly busier and noisier, crowding out the ability to create "sacred space" and time for God. Further exacerbating the dilemma of prayerlessness is the fact that a generation is growing up with more and more options for wasting time and, thus, their lives are frittered away on vanity. However, even with busy work and school schedules, most of us have more time than we realize. It is imperative that we seek to redeem this time, instead of allowing it to be squandered, along with our destinies, for the sake of entertainment and material things. Thirty-five years ago, while I was attending college, one of my leaders encouraged me to put two simple practices in place that have helped me to sustain my prayer life since that time. The first suggestion he gave me was that I should schedule a time to pray every single day. The second was to create and utilize a prayer list. Together, these two practices have strengthened my prayer life and kept me committed to prayer. How? A *schedule* determines when we will pray and helps us remain persistent. A *prayer list* gives us our focus on what to pray for.

Over the years I have talked to many who refuse to do these two things, considering them to be legalistic or "not spiritual enough," though they continued to complain about their inability to sustain their prayer life. However, in my experience as a pastor, I have found that a person struggling to maintain a life of prayer will, after implementing these two simple practices, pray ten times more than they did before.

Scheduling a Prayer Time

Try to schedule your daily prayer times during the most distraction-free hours of your day. Many find it most practical to schedule it early in the morning, before work or school, or in the evening, after all daily activities are finished. Once the prayer time has been scheduled and established, we are to consider the time "sacred," treating it as a real *appointment* with the King. By making the time *sacred*—as the time when we dialogue with the Lord—we will learn to refuse other things. For what could be more important than fellowship with Jesus?

I once received a phone call from a famous, influential person from our government. He was passing through Kansas City and had only a short window of time, but wanted to meet with me. While I deeply respected this man and would have valued meeting him, his window of opportunity for a meeting was right in the middle of my scheduled prayer time. I had made a commitment to the Lord years earlier that I would treat my prayer times as important appointments and not miss them except in the case of an emergency. When I turned down the opportunity to meet this man, he was surprised that I would not budge on my prayer time. I do not regret the opportunities that I lose because of keeping my commitment to meet with the Lord. By scheduling my times of prayer, I have found it much easier to say no to distractions, even when they seem to be important and beneficial.

Using a Prayer List

I have discovered that using a prayer list is not less spiritual, or cumbersome, but that it is a helpful tool that keeps my mind focused as I pray. Often when I do not pray with a prayer list, my mind is veering off to random subjects just five minutes into prayer. I do not always go through *every* point on my prayer list; I have the freedom to digress from my list whenever I feel inspired to do so. Overall, it is my experience that using a prayer list makes my prayer time much more focused. I have found that one of the chief reasons people cannot stay consistent in their prayer lives is the inability to focus their minds long enough to engage His presence. A prayer list helps us to remain focused on the Lord, so that we may connect with Him in a deeper way.

I have several different prayer lists that I use in my times of prayer. You can view the different prayer lists that I use in the appendix of this book. I encourage you to use these prayer lists or modify them to make them more personal for you, but, whether you use my prayer lists or not, be sure to use a prayer list to help you stay focused.

Keeping the Prophecy: Why Study and Read the Book of Revelation?

In the book of Revelation, we see the saints partnering with God in intercession to end injustice and to release His power. To most effectively partner with God at the end of the age, it is imperative that we know His heart and His plan. For this reason, a critical facet of the Sacred Charge commitment to *pray daily* is the commitment to read the book of Revelation through at least once a week. Reading and understanding the book of Revelation is not a side issue in preparing forerunners for the end of the age. While many believers relegate the book of Revelation to the sidelines of the faith because they assume that it is too difficult to understand or is irrelevant today, such thinking is an unfortunate mistake. The book of Revelation is critical to the forerunner ministry, as it reveals the very glory of Jesus and His plan to unfold the future through partnership with His people (Rev. 1:1). I refer to it as the "end-time book of Acts" and as a "canonized prayer manual" that informs us of God's plan to judge the Antichrist and his empire as He ushers in the age to come. The events of the book of Revelation will be released in a partnership between Jesus and His people, through prayer and proclamation. We must use the vital and strategic information the book gives us to equip ourselves to most effectively participate with God's plan and prepare others to do the same.

Moreover, there is a specific and unique promise of blessing in reading the book of Revelation. John writes, "Blessed is he who *reads* and those who *hear* the words of this prophecy, and *keep* those things which are written in it; for the time is near" (Rev. 1:3). For many years, I read the book of Revelation through once a week because I believed that it is a critical book for forerunners to understand. The book is very relevant and is not too difficult to understand. The main story line and structure of the book will be incredibly relevant to the generation in which the Lord returns.

Conclusion

We must be a people who *pray daily*. In praying daily, we confess our inability, incompetence, and powerlessness to fix the world. Persistent prayer releases the power of heaven to transform the problematic landscape of our cities and nations. Therefore, the *pray daily* commitment is premier in the Sacred Charge lifestyle; from this place we live out our lives. Daily prayer is a foundational building block of the forerunner ministry. A new kind of leadership is arising: before the Lord returns, our nation will be filled with churches with an established culture of prayer, led by leaders who pray.

CHAPTER 4

Fast Weekly

Positioning Ourselves to Receive More from God

T he Holy Spirit is preparing the Church for the greatest revival and the most intense pressure experienced in all of human history. Unmistakably, the Scriptures reveal that the years
preceding the Lord's return will be the Church's finest hour, as
the Bride of Christ is purified by the fires of revival and the fires
of persecution. Scripture assures us that the Bride at the end of
the age will be fully prepared for the return of Christ (Rev. 19:7).
This means that radical changes will come to the Church, as
much of what the Church accepts as normal today will be dramatically altered.

As the end of the age draws near, we must ask ourselves
how we can cooperate with the Spirit so that we may walk in the
power and intimacy with God that the New Testament church
walked in. Part of the answer is found in embracing the fasted
lifestyle and thereby positioning our hearts to receive more from
God.[1]

Fasting, in essence, is restraining some of our natural

---

[1] For more on the fasted lifestyle, see *The Rewards of Fasting* by Mike
Bickle and Dana Candler.

strengths with the purpose of positioning ourselves to receive more freely from the Spirit. Because of the hunger and physical weakness that accompanies fasting, many are afraid of it. When I first began to fast, I feared fasting. I did not like it. I rarely made it through an entire day. However, I discovered that the fear of fasting is worse than fasting itself.

Though many view fasting as archaic or even as optional, Jesus is clear that He expected believers to fast. Jesus said, "*When you fast*" (Mt. 6:17) implying that fasting was to occur in the normal course of a disciple's life. Fasting is not reserved for the "elite" Christian or for radical Christians. It is to be a part of our normal Christian life. Fasting may seem foreign and radical to some in the Western church; however, it was normal to the early church. Church history documents that fasting two days a week was a common practice for the early church, lasting hundreds of years. It is not true that the demands of our modern pace of life make fasting impractical for today.

John the Baptist is an example of one who prepared others for the coming of the Lord. John gave himself to a fasted lifestyle by distancing himself from the comforts of life, wearing simple clothing, eating the simple foods of locusts and wild honey, and at times refraining from eating and drinking (Mt. 3:1, 4; 11:18; Mk. 1:3-4, 6). John trained his disciples to live a fasted lifestyle and taught them to fast often (Mt. 9:14). As Jesus referred to John the Baptist as "the greatest man ever born of a woman" (Mt. 11:11), we can be sure that Jesus considered John's dedication to God a worthy example to follow.

In preparation for the coming of Christ, regular fasting will be a key component. Living out a fasted lifestyle is a non-negotiable and foundational aspect of every forerunner messenger's life.

Throughout history some have fasted with a wrong spirit,

seeking to earn God's favor or man's approval. This is not what God desires. God delights in our pursuit to love Him and to believe His Word. We do not fast to prove anything to God or to deserve His favor. Fasting positions our hearts to be ready and able to receive more from God, by causing us to embrace voluntary weakness in our physical body and mental ability, thereby forcing us to lean on Jesus. In this way, our hearts are positioned to receive strength from the Spirit.

There is a deep connection between food and our spirit, because our body and our spirit are dynamically connected. Although we would like to think they are separate and do not affect each other, there is a deep connection between food and the condition of our spirit, whether it is vibrant or sluggish. Godly restraint from food encourages our spirit to be more vibrant because it positions us to receive more from God.

Christianity will not have its full effect in our lives apart from the regular discipline of fasting. Jesus revealed this concept to Paul when He said "My grace is sufficient for you, for My strength is made perfect in weakness" (2 Cor. 12:9). Jesus taught Paul that embracing weakness would result in God's strength or power being perfected in his life. The release of God's power on his life was directly connected to his willingness to embrace the weakness of fasting. The physical and emotional weakness that fasting brings is challenging, as it necessitates trusting God to help us because we are incapable of functioning the way we normally would. The result is that God's strength will be manifested upon our lives in a greater way as we fast.

Do not neglect to ask for grace to strengthen you to fast. If we ask for grace to fast, we will receive it (2 Pet. 1:2; 3:18). We can be assured that He will release power to fast when we ask for it.

We can never depend on our own personal history of fasting for strength to fast, but only the strength of Christ. This means asking Him for grace before we fast and during our fast, no matter how short or long it may be. The release of God's grace does not mean the alleviation of tiredness or hunger, but the strength to be resolved to continue in the fast. Grace for fasting is what happens when the Lord strengthens our determination, so that we follow through more consistently on the fasts we set our hearts to do.

Seven Reasons to Fast in Scripture

Jesus emphasized that the Father will reward fasting, saying "when you fast . . . your Father who sees in secret will *reward you openly*" (Mt. 6:17-18). The Father is watching us with fixed attention when we fast, and it is His desire to respond to us by rewarding us, for He "is a rewarder of those who diligently seek Him" (Heb. 11:6). Some of the rewards are external, meaning our circumstances are touched by God's power and favor. Some of the rewards are internal, meaning God touches our hearts in new depths. In other words, we fast both to walk in more of God's power to change the world and to encounter more of His heart to change our hearts. From Scripture, I present seven different rewards, or reasons to fast.

1. Fasting to Experience the Power of God in Our Ministry

Probably, the most common reason that people fast is to experience more of the power of God in their personal ministry. Jesus pointed His disciples to fasting and prayer when they could not deliver a demonized boy. When they asked Jesus why the boy was not delivered, He replied, "This kind does not go out except by prayer and fasting" (Mt. 17:21). There is a dimension of power that is only released through regular prayer and fasting.

The power of John the Baptist's preaching was undoubtedly connected to his fasted lifestyle.

Many who led revivals through history fasted regularly. For example, John Wesley and George Whitefield were used dramatically by the Lord in England and America during the First Great Awakening of the 1700s. Thousands were saved and England was set ablaze under their anointed preaching. When they came to America, the spirit of revival followed, touching the nation through the anointed preaching of people like David Brainerd, Jonathan Edwards, and others. They were all committed to regular fasting. John Wesley fasted on Wednesdays and Fridays each week, and challenged his preachers to also fast two days a week. He became an organizer of the revival, sending thousands of circuit preachers to travel by horseback and preach from town to town. Wesley is quoted as saying: "The man that never fasts is no more on the way to heaven than the man that never prays." These revivalists understood the dynamic connection between fasting and preaching with authority.

John G. Lake is another example of a man who was dedicated to fasting and prayer and saw the power of God released upon His ministry in a unique way. Lake, who died in 1935, was a wealthy businessman from Chicago who became gripped with a vision to operate in the power of God to heal the sick. He deeply desired to experience power like the early apostles. Therefore, he sought the Lord through fasting and prayer until he experienced it. When preaching in South Africa, in just a five-year time span he saw over 500,000 documented healings ranging from the raising of the dead to paralytics being healed and blind eyes opening. He saw thousands upon thousands of new converts and hundreds of new churches. Other than the first apostles, I know of no other ministry in history where the power of God was so dynamically released. Lake was a man deeply committed to fasting and prayer, who urged others to do likewise.

2. Fasting for the Fulfillment of God's Promises to a Geographic Region

The Lord has prophetic plans and promises for each city and nation that will only be fully released when His people pray and fast for their release. God's promises are not guarantees. Rather, they are prophetic invitations to respond to God and cooperate with Him so that He will release the plans of His heart. Prophetic promises are invitations to cry out in faith for their fulfillment.

Daniel prayed and fasted for the fulfillment of God's promise to release Israel from captivity and return to their land (Neh. 1:4; 9:1). Although the promise was given, the prophet faithfully prayed and fasted that it would come to pass. Nehemiah also gave himself to fasting and prayer for the release of God's promises to his generation, and the Lord answered Him only after he was faithful to ask for them (Neh. 1:4; 9:1). Cornelius also fasted and prayed for the heart of God to be released, and he saw the salvation of his entire household and a door of grace open for the Gentiles to be saved (Acts 10:1-4, 30, 44-45). Likewise, the promises of God over our families, cities, and nations will come to pass as the Bride of Christ cries out to God with prayers and fasting.

3. Fasting to Stop a Crisis

Fasting to seek God for mercy during a personal and even a national crisis is seen throughout Scripture. Hannah, the mother of Samuel, sought the Lord through prayer and fasting in order to end her personal crisis of barrenness (1 Sam. 1:7). The Lord answered her cry by giving her a son who grew up to become a prophet to Israel. Crying out to God with fasting and prayer was a catalyst to God answering this crisis in Hannah's life.

Fasting is also used by God to stop a national crisis. On various occasions, God reversed Israel's desperate situation after they turned to Him in corporate prayer and fasting (Joel 2:12-17). When Joel prophesied about God's coming judgments over the nation of Israel, he called Israel to turn to God through prayer and fasting in the hope that He would relent from judgment. Joel prophesied that God would judge Israel using locusts, and then later by Nebuchadnezzar's Babylonian army. On both occasions, Joel called Israel to turn to God in prayer and fasting (Joel 1:2-18; 2:1-9, 12-15).

Our nation today is in the midst of a crisis that no one has power to alleviate apart from the favor and power of God that is released in part through corporate fasting and prayer. The crisis in our nation includes increased abortion rates, the attacks on the sanctity of marriage, the rise of radical Islam, economic pressures, and the massive trend toward compromise that is occurring in the Church. Compromise and lethargy in the Church heightens every other problem. Many are polluting the doctrine of the grace of God as they yield to the fear of man with a man-pleasing spirit. They are removing the offense of the gospel by presenting the grace of God as that which empowers people to feel good while they are sinning, without calling them to genuine repentance. The only remedy for the Church is God's mercy to revive us with His powerful presence. Therefore, we must continue to beseech Him with fasting and prayer. We recall the days of Jonah, when Nineveh repented with fasting and received great mercy from God (Jon. 3:3-9).

4. Fasting for Prophetic Revelation of the End Times

Another biblical reason to give ourselves to the fasted lifestyle is to receive greater insight into the Scriptures that pertain to the end times. Through prayer and fasting, the prophet Daniel was given increased revelation to understand end-time events, especially related to Israel's end-time destiny. Daniel writes his account by saying, "I set my face toward the Lord God to make request *by prayer and supplications, with fasting* . . . while I was speaking . . . Gabriel . . . talked with me, and said, 'O Daniel, I have now come forth to give you *skill to understand* . . . understand the vision'" (Dan. 9:3, 21-23).

As Daniel fasted and prayed, the angel Gabriel came to him to reveal events that would happen in the generation when the Lord returns. Daniel was given skill to understand events related to Christ's return. Again, in Daniel chapter 10, following a twenty-one-day fast, an angel appeared to Daniel to give him understanding of end-time events. The angel told him, "From the first day that you set your heart to understand . . . your words were heard; and I have come because of your words" (Dan. 10:12).

The Scriptures foretell an unprecedented release of prophetic revelation during the generation of the Lord's return. In Acts 2, we know that Peter pointed to this reality when he quoted the prophet Joel, who declared, "It shall come to pass *afterward* that I will pour out My Spirit on all flesh; your sons and your daughters shall prophesy, your old men shall dream dreams, and also on My menservants and on My maidservants I will pour out My Spirit *in those days*" (Joel 2:28-29). The "afterward" in this passage speaks of the concerts of prayer in which the people were to regularly fast and cry out to God in Joel 2:12-17.

Daniel prophesied that God would raise up people with prophetic understanding who would teach multitudes (Dan. 11:33-35). It is revealed that these people will have mature understanding of what God is doing at the end of the age (Jer. 23:18-20).

For those who feel called to be an end-times messenger,

regular fasting is a non-negotiable essential element of their preparation. The forerunner calling is not only for preachers—many will instruct others through dance, drama, art, writing, and music. With the Internet and modern technology, some who have never preached a sermon may write an email or make a podcast that will impact an entire nation with prophetic insight into a key end-time event. Those of us who are desiring to be forerunner messengers must fast regularly, that we may be ready to receive revelation to instruct many in the days preceding Christ's return.

5. Fasting for Protection

A fifth biblical purpose for fasting is for protection. Before Ezra led a group of Jews from Babylon back to Israel to help rebuild their nation, he fasted and prayed to God for protection on the journey (Ezra 8:21-23). The trip from Babylon to Israel was a dangerous walk that covered nearly 700 miles. They needed divine protection from thieves and bandits on the road as many were killed or robbed on such a journey. Ezra gathered the people to fast and pray for the protection of God upon the people and upon their supplies.

Esther also called the Jews in Persia to fast for divine protection (Esth. 4:16). A decree to kill all of the Jews in Persia had been set in motion and Esther knew that their only hope would be the divine intervention of God through fasting and prayer (Esth. 3:13, 4:7). Esther first needed protection for herself, because she was going to approach the king without a royal summons in order to appeal the death decree over her people. At the time, the law of land gave a penalty of death for those who approached the king uninvited, and many fasted and prayed for Esther's life as she challenged the law (Esth. 4:16). Through the fasting of the Jews, the Lord spared Esther's life and then reversed the plans of Haman to exterminate all the Jewish people in the land of Persia (Esth. 9:1).

6. Fasting for Direction

Fasting for direction has many biblical precedents. Throughout the New Testament, the early church fasted for divine direction. Paul and others fasted and prayed for direction over their ministry and before selecting and commissioning elders of the new churches in Lystra, Iconium, and Antioch (Acts 13:1-2; 14:21, 23). God will give more direction if we fast and pray and ask Him for it. This includes direction for our life, our family, our ministry, or our assignment in the marketplace. Rather than anxiously wondering what the will of God is for our lives, we should take confidence in His desire to answer and respond to us when we seek Him through fasting and prayer.

7. Fasting to Grow in Intimacy with Jesus

Finally, there is the biblical purpose for fasting to grow in intimacy with Jesus. This is what I refer to as the Bridegroom fast. The Bridegroom fast is not for an external reward, but for the internal reward of growing in intimacy with Jesus.

This kind of fasting is motivated by our desire for Jesus rather than by our desire for more power in ministry, or to be delivered from a personal crisis. The Bridegroom fast is a fast to come before Jesus as our Bridegroom King. This fast is primarily centered on desire—understanding both God's desire for us and awakening our desire for Him.

The description of Jesus as the Bridegroom God implies that He is the God of desire and that His desire is toward us. Jesus is not only the King, with power to change circumstances; He is also the Bridegroom with power to change and touch our hearts.

As sons of God, we are in the position to experience the power of God's throne. As the Bride of Christ, we are in the position to experience the desires of God's heart. We give ourselves to fasting because we want to feel God's desire for us and we want to increasingly desire Him.

Understanding the Bridegroom Fast

When Jesus first spoke to me about the Bridegroom fast, it was a major paradigm shift for me. Every other fast is for the purpose of experiencing external reward, such as more power in ministry, but the Bridegroom fast is solely motivated by desire for Jesus.

Matthew reports that the disciples of John approached Jesus, asking, "Why do we and the Pharisees fast often, but Your disciples do not fast?" And Jesus said to them, "Can the friends of the Bridegroom mourn as long as the Bridegroom is with them? But the days will come when the Bridegroom will be taken away from them, and then they will fast" (Mt. 9:14-15).

The first time that Jesus described Himself as the Bridegroom God was in the context of teaching on fasting. This passage reminds us of Isaiah's teaching on the emotions of God as a bridegroom, describing God as delighting in His people and rejoicing over them as a bridegroom rejoices over his bride (Isa. 62:4-5). Jesus introduced Himself as the Bridegroom God, as the One who delighted in and rejoiced over His disciples.

Jesus answered the question concerning his disciples' lack of fasting by saying, "Can the friends of the bridegroom *mourn* as long as the bridegroom is with them?" (Mt. 9:15). The disciples enjoyed Jesus' presence. They felt delight in being in Jesus' company, knowing that He took pleasure in His relationship with them. While Jesus, the Bridegroom God, was in the presence of

His disciples, they were not to mourn with fasting.

Jesus went on to say, "But the days will come when the bridegroom will be taken away from them, and *then they will fast*" (Mt. 9:15). Jesus was to be taken away from His disciples in His death on the cross. At that time, the joy that they experienced in their nearness to Jesus would be turned to mourning, or longing, for His presence to return. When Jesus died, the disciples were heartsick and fasted with mourning to experience the same closeness of His presence. It was then that they fasted with the same consistency and intensity of John's disciples.

Through Jesus' death and resurrection, He established the new covenant in which His Spirit would dwell in each believer. The good news is that Jesus' disciples throughout church history have been able to experience the nearness of His presence by the indwelling Spirit. Now, with Jesus physically gone, we fast to position our hearts to encounter Him in a greater measure. We know the painful longing to be closer to Him. When we engage in this fast, Jesus will release revelation concerning how He feels about us, His disciples.

We mourn because we are discontent with our current experience of nearness to Jesus. We refuse to accept spiritual dullness. Fasting before our Bridegroom God is a catalyst to increase the depth and the measure in which we receive from Jesus. We receive a greater measure of revelation of Jesus, at an accelerated pace, and with a deeper impact on our heart. In other words, by fasting, we receive more, we receive it faster, and it touches us more deeply.

Seeking Jesus in the Bridegroom fast strengthens our sense of identity as a cherished bride before Jesus. This, in turn, transforms our emotions. We experience the internal reward of having an identity that is rooted in the knowledge of God's affection for us.

With the revelation of Jesus with the heart of a bridegroom, we have greater confidence in His presence. Because we feel enjoyed by Him, we press in with greater consistency to be near Him. The tenderness of Jesus' heart for us makes us tender in love back to Him. As our hearts are tenderized, we make different choices, leading to different outcomes in the places we go, the people we meet, and the things we do. Thus, it affects how we spend our time and money, who we marry, how we raise children, and what focus we have in ministry. Our sinful desires are transformed by a greater desire to be near Jesus and to walk in obedience to Him.

Practical Issues Related to Fasting

As you embark upon your journey in fasting, it is important to become familiar with the practical issues related to fasting. Fasting was designed to be a consistent part of our lives. We should see it as a gift from God. From a desire to see God's people encounter His passionate heart for them, I urge those who are physically healthy to fast at least one day a week. I challenge those with a forerunner messenger calling to follow the example of many through church history who fasted two days a week. It will position our heart to experience more of the affections of Jesus.

I suggest five different fasts that we may participate in. The first is a *regular fast*, which entails going without food and drinking only water, or liquid that has very little or no calories. The second is a *liquid fast*, which is going without solid food and drinking only light liquids, such as fruit and vegetable juices. Third, the *partial fast* includes abstaining from tasty foods and eating only vegetables or nuts. This was the fast chosen by Daniel, who ate only vegetables and drank only water (Dan. 1:12). Fourth, the *Benedict fast* was established by Saint Benedict and consisted of eating only one meal a day. Lastly, the *absolute fast*, or Esther fast, includes abstaining from food and water. This fast should only be participated in with extreme caution, as going without water should never be done for more than one to three days.

The level at which a person engages in fasting from food should be determined according to age and with regard to any physical illness or limitations. Those with a known or suspected physical disability or illness, or with any history of an eating disorder, should never fast except in consultation with and under the supervision of a qualified physician. Children are also discouraged from fasting food and should never engage in a fast without express parental consent and oversight. Minors who desire to fast should consider non-food abstentions, such as TV, movies, Internet surfing, video games, and other forms of entertainment. The Bible does not call children to fast.

If you are healthy and at an age that enables you to fast, fasting actually leads to making your body healthier and changes what you desire to eat and drink. Participation in regular fasting as a lifestyle necessitates a healthy lifestyle on days when you are eating, and should include exercise and a proper diet. A fasted lifestyle includes a disciplined life in which we steward our bodies and time with wisdom. As we continue to give ourselves to the Bridegroom fast, our desire to live a healthy lifestyle and be intentional about stewarding our bodies and time will naturally increase.

When we become jealous for impact on our spirit, living out the fasted lifestyle is essential to position ourselves to receive more freely from God. As we embark on the seven commitments of a forerunner, let us join together in beseeching God for the grace of fasting that transforms us, impacts the world around us, and leads to a love encounter with Jesus the Bridegroom. May we ask Him for help, knowing that He will strengthen our hearts to fast and prepare us to encounter the presence of Jesus through His Spirit living within us. My prayer is that each person seeking to live out the sacred charge as a forerunner would set their hearts to walk out the fasted lifestyle and to encounter more of the love of Jesus.

CHAPTER 5

Do Justly

Being Zealous for Good Works that Exalt Jesus

Anyone reading the newspapers today realizes that we are in desperate need of God's justice being established on the earth. Abortion, poverty, world hunger, racism, disease, and countless other crises that plague this generation clearly reveal our critical need for a deliverer. Jesus calls His Church to respond to the challenge of systemic injustice that afflicts the nations. Micah the prophet famously thundered God's requirement of all who seek to love God wholeheartedly, "He has shown you, O man, what is good; and what does the Lord require of you but to *do justly*, to *love mercy*, and to *walk humbly* with your God?" (Mic. 6:8). Micah's prophetic declaration reveals how God wants us to live and what He requires from us. We are called to be workers of justice and lovers of mercy, with a spirit of humility. Loving people by doing justly is the *visible* measurement of our *invisible* (but real) love for God. It is impossible for us to say that we love Jesus without loving people by doing justly in mercy and compassion to people in need (1 Jn. 3:17-19; 4:20).

From a New Testament point of view, to do justly involves being zealous for good works that exalt Jesus. We manifest our love for God as we serve people by doing works of justice and compassion that help the poor, the fatherless, and the oppressed, and by working to impact the seven spheres of society, which are family; education; government (politics, law, and military); economy (business, science, and technology); arts (entertainment and sports); media; and religion.

The Call to Do Justly and to Love Mercy

The call to give ourselves to works of justice is a call to exalt Jesus and give expression to His message to love people. Christ redeemed us "that He might . . . purify for Himself His own *special* people, *zealous for good works*" (Titus 2:14). One of the glorious results of receiving salvation is found in being set apart by God as a vessel that manifests Jesus' love to the nations. We are motivated to do these works out of the revelation of how special we are to God. This ignites zeal in our hearts to do works of justice and compassion that exalt Jesus and bring people to Him.

There is more involved than only doing good humanitarian works to help people. These are works that flow out of the revelation that we are dear to God and that the people we help are dear to God. There is a spiritual dimension to these works of justice and compassion. It involves being intentional about doing good works on a regular basis because they please God and make people more aware of His love and kindness.

Works of justice include feeding the poor, and caring for the needy, orphans, widows, and homeless. It also includes alleviating the oppression of abortion, poverty, misogyny, and racism in the marketplace, law enforcement, education, and employment arenas, and many other issues. When we encounter God's heart for us and His heart for justice, these works of justice become a priority to us in the use of our time, finances, and energy. A commitment to do justly is costly. It is inconvenient, but it is worth it.

Gaining revelation of the way Jesus feels about us as His people who are special to Him gives great dignity to our good works. It transforms them from a dutiful responsibility to being an expression of our deep relationship with Him. They communicate that God is loving and good and that He desires people to receive His love and goodness. It energizes us to see that our good works help others to receive the love of Jesus. Being used by God as vessels of love gives us even more motivation to be intentional about doing good works, even when it is inconvenient and costly to do so.

We love God by helping to meet the needs of the people He loves. As we do this, we become visible signs of the invisible love of God for mankind. Works of justice and compassion become our visible message of love toward God as we exclaim, "Behold what manner of love the Father has bestowed on us, that we should be called children of God!" (1 Jn. 3:1). Our works become an invitation to the world to become His beloved children. Our very works declare that we dwell in the love of God. "But whoever has this world's goods, and sees his brother in need, and shuts up his heart from him, how does the love of God abide in him?" (1 Jn. 3:17). When unbelievers see the testimony of our good works, it exalts Jesus. Why? It demonstrates His power to transform our hearts from selfishness as we touch others in the overflow of grateful love.

Peter stressed this point to the Church, revealing that we are "His own *special* people, that you may proclaim the praises of Him . . . when they speak against you as evildoers, they may, *by your good works* which they observe, glorify God" (1 Pet. 2:9-15). We are called to make God's reputation known among unbelievers by the works of justice and compassion that we give ourselves to.

In part, God entrusts His name, or reputation, to what His people do. The way we live our lives relays a message to the world about who God is and what He is like. When we obey Him, His name is honored and glorified. When we do not, it dishonors and misrepresents His good name (2 Sam. 12:14; Rom. 2:24). As we serve the people around us, we declare that our God is kind and that He is involved in the affairs of real people.

Peter goes on to say, "They speak against you as *evildoers*" (1 Pet. 2:12). As we declare God's name, we must be prepared to face opposition, even as we do good works. When we proclaim the goodness of God and how He has changed our lives, it will offend some who refuse to acknowledge His greatness. Some unbelievers are naturally suspicious and critical of believers. They accuse the Church of being no different from themselves. They believe that our message is wrong and that we have evil motives behind the good works that we do.

God uses our good works to open the hearts of some unbelievers. Peter continues, "When they speak against you as evildoers, they may, *by your good works* which they observe, glorify God" (1 Pet. 2:12). Even when many resist our proclamation of the gospel, some will change their resistant attitude and open their heart to the love of God if we back our message up with a lifestyle of loving people in practical ways. If we remain consistent in doing good works, over time many will come into the kingdom. Good works are the proof of the message that God really is good and that He is pursuing a relationship with those who need to accept the gospel.

The Holy Spirit is not only calling us to do good works, but to love mercy and embody a spirit of humility as we pursue justice and works of compassion (Mic. 6:8). God's plan is to silence the accusation of men against Jesus and His Church by His people consistently doing deeds of justice with an attitude of meekness. Peter makes it known: "This is the will of God, that by doing good you may put to silence the ignorance of foolish men" (1 Pet. 2:15). Works of justice that are done in a right spirit will eventually triumph over the false accusations against God and His people.

Maintaining consistency and longevity in doing good works is an essential component in impacting them with the love of God. Unbelievers accuse God of being indifferent to the suffering that is in the world. God has chosen to answer these accusations against Him by empowering His people to consistently serve those in need.

It makes a big statement when people selflessly serve others. When we transcend the urge for selfishness, as we sacrificially love others, some unbelievers will conclude that God's love and transforming power is real. Instead of seeing God as unkind and indifferent to the suffering that is present in our broken world, they see Him as involved. Unbelievers take notice when God's people consistently do good works in a way that costs them real time and money, while at the same time being kind to those who accuse them.

Believers are to be known by what they do, instead of by what they do not do. It is not enough to avoid scandalous sin with moral behavior. It is when we are actively engaged in works of justice that unbelievers listen to our message and acknowledge that God is not distant and indifferent, but is committed to the world and active in the lives of people. Over time, works of justice will triumph over the accusations of the enemy and lead many to Jesus. We give ourselves to works of justice "that they may see your good works and glorify your Father in heaven" (Mt. 5:16).

Doing Justly to Prepare for the Return of Christ

Works of justice that exalt Jesus are a primary function of the forerunner ministry, as we learn from the life of John the Baptist. The messenger who prepared the way for the first coming of Jesus prepared people to receive Jesus by calling them to live lives of justice and mercy. Before Jesus returns to the earth and establishes His justice, His messengers will go before Him to prepare people to receive Him. As we live lives of justice and call others to do the same, we prepare the Church to partner with Jesus as He returns to establish His kingdom.

There is only one place in the New Testament where we see details of the message that John proclaimed to prepare the way for Jesus as Messiah. Luke tells us that the people asked John how to live their lives in a way that prepared for the coming of the king.

> The people asked him, saying, "What shall we do then?" [John] answered and said to them, "He who has two tunics, let him give to him who has none; and he who has food, let him do likewise." Then tax collectors . . . said to him, "Teacher, what shall we do?" He said, "Collect no more than what is appointed for you." Likewise the soldiers asked him, saying, "Teacher, what shall we do?" So he said to them, "Do not intimidate anyone or accuse falsely, and be content with your wages."
>
> —Luke 3:10-14

In essence, John called the people to live lives of justice and mercy. Throughout Luke 3, John spoke to three different groups: the multitudes (all people in general), tax collectors (those involved in finances), and soldiers (those with authority in society). To each group, he gave different applications of the same principle "to do justly, to love mercy, and to walk humbly with God." To the multitudes, John explained that practically walking out the message of justice is to share our resources in a practical way. He explained that if you have an extra jacket or extra food, you should give it away. Many in the West have more than one jacket, but how many of us have actually given one away before it gets old or before it is unwanted? Now, this may seem unpractical or just foolhardy sentiment, but if we are serious about doing justly, these are the questions that we must ask. There is a huge difference between simply hearing a message about justice and actually engaging with the Lord and doing justly as the Scripture defines it. Nonetheless, we must challenge our own assumptions as we seek to walk out the Scriptures.

To those with financial influence, John taught them to always do what was just and merciful. Today's culture has embraced a value that says if we can cheat people out of a little money by selling something for more than its worth or buying something for less than its fair value, it is an admirable skill. John challenged the faithful to not make decisions that took advantage of another's lack of knowledge or unfortunate life position. Do not extort money from people beyond that which is truly just. We are to be honest with people in our financial dealings with them. We do what is right, not just what is expedient and what we can get away with. This means that we must make just decisions, even if we lose some of the money we could have gained if we had put a twist on the information or used just a little deceit.

The soldiers in that day kept the order in society much like police officers do today. They had authority in society and power over others. John demanded that they use their influence to bring about goodness and justice. Whether it is a police force, a business, or a ministry, it is imperative that we walk in truth and humility, preferring others and serving those who are weak. We are not to intimidate people to fulfill our own agenda, but we are to use our authority to bring about good in the lives of others. If God has established you in a position of authority, one purpose is to make known His heart of justice and mercy to those under your authority.

The Foundation of Justice Is Night and Day Prayer

Jesus walked upon the earth as the image of the invisible God. One way that He expressed Micah's message to do justly and love mercy was in teaching on the power of prayer that brings about justice. Jesus encouraged His followers by saying, "Shall not God bring about justice for His elect, who cry to Him day and night . . .? I tell you that He will bring about justice for them speedily" (Lk. 18:7-8, NAS).

Jesus taught that our works of justice will be most effective when they are rooted in night and day prayer. We must never substitute prayer for works of justice, or substitute works of justice for prayer. Both are very important in the kingdom of God. From heaven's perspective, they are two sides of the same coin and must go hand-in-hand. Prayers for justice must be followed by works of justice. When we cry out for justice in intercession, we change the spiritual atmosphere in the area in which the injustice is occurring. By praying for justice to be established, we release an increase of God's power in the midst of our works of justice. The result is a greater release of God's presence in the context of our good works. Through prayer we confront the demonic forces behind the injustice (Eph. 6:12).

Healing the sick person is even better than giving them money to go to the doctor. Breaking demonic oppression off people is even better than listening with compassion to their battle against oppression. In order to walk in the greatest expression of justice, prayer and works must move together as one reality.

The humanitarian movement overlooks prayer as being foundational for justice because they do not see the demonic powers that lie behind much of the injustice that occurs in the earth. It is important to minister to physical, economic, and medical needs. However, the Holy Spirit is willing to also release power through us—power that removes the demonic influence that perpetuates injustice.

Another aspect of combining prayer with works of justice is that the one who does the work is replenished by the love of God because they spend time in God's presence when praying. This empowers them to love others. Regularly experiencing God's love empowers us to love others more consistently. Intimacy with Jesus through prayer is key to ministry without burnout. Connecting with the Spirit helps us to sustain a life of good works without burning out after a few years. Jesus said that we cannot do anything apart from connecting with Him. Jesus declared, "I am the vine, you are the branches. He who abides in Me, and I in him, bears much fruit; *for without Me you can do nothing*" (Jn. 15:5). Prayer is indispensable in empowering us to love God and people better.

Prayer is also foundational for justice in helping us maintain allegiance to Jesus in our works of justice. We must be zealous for good works on His terms and for His reasons. A false justice movement is emerging in the Church—a movement of humanitarian efforts that undermines the truth about Jesus. It is rooted in humanism and rejects the absolute truths of Scripture. It is a counterfeit movement that is occurring under the banner of the kingdom of God. Many involved in this false justice movement are sincere about their mission.

Works of Justice with Love for Mercy

Just as good works remain incomplete without prayer, so prayer is incomplete without good works. It is imperative that works go forth from a foundation of prayer, and that prayer is given expression with good works. Worship is love in action. The worship that moves God's heart flows from believers whose hearts are moved by the needy. As we worship, we connect songs of love to Jesus with acts of love to the needy. The clearest instruction concerning the relationship of fasting and prayer to justice is found in Isaiah 58:1-12. It outlines practical ways to do works of justice with a spirit of mercy and humility.

At a time when Israel seemed to be seeking God, Isaiah was sent as God's messenger to tell them that seeking Him without helping others was not pleasing to Him. They felt satisfied and justified in only seeking God, without embracing works of justice and mercy. God wanted more than their worship songs. The Lord thundered through Isaiah:

> Tell My people their transgression . . . they seek Me daily, and delight to know My ways...they take delight in approaching God. "Why have we fasted," they say, "and You have not seen? Why have we afflicted our souls, and You take no notice?"
>
> —Isaiah 58:1-3

The nation of Israel was seeking God daily in prayer with

fasting, they claimed to delight in knowing God's ways through studying the Scriptures, and they even took pleasure in approaching God's presence. Although these are good qualities, the Lord viewed their lifestyle as sinful, because their attitude was wrong and they did not follow through with works of justice.

When Israel asked the Lord why He had not answered their prayers and days of fasting, He revealed that their attitude was wrong and that they had stopped short of actually worshiping Him by ignoring acts of justice. He said, "In the day of your fast . . . you exploit all your laborers. Indeed you fast for strife and debate, and to strike with the fist of wickedness" (Isa. 58:3-4). The leaders of Israel fasted to gain God's favor on their business and to appear devout. But in reality they were exploiting the very ones that God placed under them. They used God's favor on their life to their own advancement, without helping the needy. The business leaders of that day used their influence and resources as a means to increase their personal comfort without giving any of their finances to the needy. However, God had released His blessing on them so that they could use their influence to mobilize more people in good works that would exalt the Lord by helping the oppressed.

Our resources and influence may be small, but we can still use them to mobilize others for works of justice. The way we steward the small amount of resource and influence that God gives us today is a picture of the way we will steward a great increase in the future. To him who is faithful with little, God will give increase and make him ruler over much more.

The Lord continued to reveal His heart to Israel by explaining that the approach to fasting and prayer that is pleasing to Him is one that is joined with works of justice. The Lord answered them by saying, "Is this not the fast that I have chosen: to loose the bonds of wickedness, to undo the heavy burdens, to let the oppressed go free, and that you break every yoke?" (Isa. 58:6).

Removing bonds of wickedness, heavy burdens, and yokes means relieving people from the bondage that results from oppressive laws and social barriers that have been created over decades and sometimes even centuries. It speaks of the systemic injustice in society that has institutionalized wickedness. There are cultural mindsets that are the result of educational disadvantages, lack of preventative or appropriate health care, or legal inequalities and other developments that affect individuals in a negative way. The collective impact of these mindsets and social conditions keeps many individuals in bondage. Whether it is the inner city, the immigrant community, in a school system, or any other part of society, God calls us to do our part in helping others. Removing heavy burdens includes training others in life skills that allow them to live successfully as individuals and not as dependents of a state system.

We will not alleviate all social injustice on earth until Jesus returns. However, when we combine prayer with works of justice, many will be helped. We can make a difference now. We can change the world now before the Lord returns. After He returns, He will complete the work that we are doing when He causes justice to fill the whole earth.

As we work to change oppressive laws and unjust social barriers, we must meet some of the practical needs of those who are waiting for change. In other words, we meet needs now while waiting for certain laws to change. Along with a vision for societal change, we must see and serve the needs of those individuals awaiting freedom by sharing our resources of food, housing, and clothing with them. The fast that God has chosen is to share our bread with the hungry, to bring the poor into our house, and to provide clothing for them (Isa. 58:7).

As we work to meet the needs of those suffering from injustice, it is essential that we serve in a spirit of humility by treating the oppressed with dignity and respect. There is no formula for interpreting suffering. We cannot understand the complexities that have developed over decades, nor can we fully understand another's life situation. The Lord instructs us to "take away the yoke from your midst, the pointing of the finger, and speaking wickedness" (Isa. 58:9).

When serving the needs of the afflicted, we must not point the finger by judging where they went wrong or how they got into the situation they are in. The greatest minds cannot figure out all of the reasons and complexities that contribute to their difficult life circumstances. Our role is to love and serve them with humility instead of thinking we have accurately analyzed their situation. We must not serve the oppressed with a spirit of judgment and criticism in our heart. The oppressed can easily discern when people are helping them in a spirit of humility and acceptance or in a spirit of pride with judgment. We must see the dignity of individuals who are being oppressed in order to serve them and show that God loves them.

God will release a supernatural dimension of His power when fasting and prayer are joined to works of justice. The Lord promised to back up prayer and works of justice with His presence when He declared,

> Then your light shall break forth like the morning, your healing shall spring forth speedily, and your righteousness shall go before you; the glory of the LORD shall be your rear guard. Then you shall call, and the LORD will answer . . . The LORD will guide you continually, and satisfy

your soul in drought, and strengthen your bones.

—Isaiah 58:8-9, 11

Consistent prayer will result in the increase of God's power and presence when it is connected to works of justice. The glory of God will be present on our lives as He causes light to break forth that removes bondage and empowers the very ones who work for justice to walk in the new dimensions of freedom, called righteousness. The Lord will guide us prophetically, answer us when we call on Him, satisfy our soul with intimacy, and strengthen our bones with physical healing.

Setting Our Hearts to Do Justly

We will never meet all of the needs in our hurting world, but together we can make an impact on the lives of some by consistently doing small acts of compassion. Impacting the lives of a few, in turn, will impact the lives of many over time. If we ask, God will give us creative ideas about how we can help those who are oppressed. He takes delight in us when we dream big and think outside the box. Do not be limited to what is currently being done on the organizational chart of the ministry you are a part of. God may give you an entirely new idea that reaches people who are outside the reach of the ministry that others are currently doing. God is raising up courageous people who will do great exploits without being intimidated by obstacles. Let us join together in giving ourselves to prayer and justice on God's terms, for "we are His workmanship, created in Christ Jesus for good works, which God prepared beforehand that we should walk in them" (Eph. 2:10).

CHAPTER 6
Give Extravagantly
The Joy of Financial Power Encounters

The Divine Challenge

The Holy Spirit is raising up more and more people who have set their heart to give financially to the kingdom in an extravagant way. He is calling many to financially support works of justice and, specifically, to support the prayer movement, which is at the very heart of the end-time justice movement.

There is only one place in all of Scripture where God challenges us to test Him. The Lord says,

> Bring all the tithes into the storehouse, that there may be food in My house, and *try Me,* now in this . . . if I will not *open for you the windows of heaven* and pour out for you such blessing that there will not be room enough to receive it.
>
> —Malachi 3:10

In the area of giving money, God challenges us to give extravagantly. He promises to extravagantly answer our giving. It stirs our faith when this happens. I refer to this as entering into the *joy of financial power encounters*. The Father beckons His children to test Him in their giving; it is as if He is saying "Wait and see what I will do! Watch Me open up the very storehouse of heaven to bless you!" Giving extravagantly is the condition that God requires for all who desire to take hold of His promise to release finances in a supernatural way.

In Malachi 3, the Lord called us to give Him the tithe of all our money by giving a tenth of our money to support His kingdom. Tithing is the entry point for experiencing the joy of financial power encounters in an ongoing way. Put simply, tithing is basic Christianity. To tithe is to trust God directly with 10 percent of our money.

When we give 10 percent of our income to God, we position ourselves to receive financial blessing. We have a greater buying power on 90 percent of our money with God's blessing because of tithing than we have on 100 percent of it without God's blessing when we don't tithe. In other words, when we give 10 percent to the Lord, He causes our 90 percent to go farther than the 100 percent when we don't give to Him. He delights in multiplying our finances back to us. God will directly respond to our giving by opening the financial windows of heaven over us.

He wants us to trust His leadership over our finances; He desires that we would give with confidence that He is watching and will be involved in our finances in a supernatural way. Those who make the Sacred Charge commitments will give beyond their tithe. Giving extravagantly implies that we give above and beyond 10 percent of our finances to the Lord.

When God supernaturally answers our giving, it fills us with joy. In other words, He sometimes responds to us by giving us an amount of money that directly corresponds to an amount we gave. He takes pleasure in doing this because it develops our relationship with Him by letting us know that He is watching and is involved with us in our giving.

When we see the cause and effect dynamic between our giving and His return on our giving, it powerfully touches our heart.

Power encounters in finances occur when we give to the kingdom, and God returns it to us in an unexpected way, but in a way that corresponds to the amount we gave. As we enter into God's challenge to give, we embark on an exhilarating adventure by going outside our comfort zone as we test Him. Giving, and then watching His supernatural response, ushers us into new depths of our relationship with God.

Extravagant Giving unto Intimacy with God

For many years, I have encouraged people to give beyond their tithe. I like calling people to give extravagantly because I know that they will experience God's supernatural involvement in their finances.

I will share a few testimonies from my personal experience in the hope of encouraging you to accept God's challenge to test Him in your finances. He will answer in a way that will make it clear that He is watching our giving. When we are aware that God's eyes are on us with pleasure, we view giving as a relational adventure with God. Giving is a birthing ground for intimacy with Jesus. Jesus taught, "When you do a charitable deed, your Father who *sees* in secret will reward you openly" (Matt. 6:3-4). When the Lord responds to our giving by returning finances back to us, the most exciting part is not in receiving more money, but in knowing that the God of the universe is watching us! He cares enough to pay attention to the details of our lives and respond to us. This deeply touches our hearts.

As we remain consistent in extravagant giving, we will

develop a personal history with God in the realm of our finances. This is a dynamic part of our spiritual life and plays a key role in our spiritual vitality. Our hearts are more deeply connected to our finances that most of us know. It affects some of the level of our intimacy with Him. Many love Jesus but they do not venture out in faith in the area of giving. They miss out on experiencing intimacy with God in their finances.

As forerunners, we want to develop a history in our finance that makes us confident that God is intimately watching our heart and our money.

When I was 18 years old, my youth group was leading many people to the Lord. Our new believers did not have Bibles, so I decided to buy a couple hundred Bibles to give to each person who had become a Christian. The only problem was that I did not have any money. I only made $30 a week and I had given most of it to the kingdom week by week! The Bibles cost $301.24, ten times my weekly income. I had never done anything like this before, but I felt a strong leading from the Lord to order the Bibles and believe Him for the finances to come, knowing that I had been giving my money to His kingdom. I had never supernaturally received this much money from the Lord. I decided to tell God of my need and no one else. I believed that He would respond to me.

In my excitement I began to tell many of the new believers about the Bibles that were coming for them. I prayed and waited for the finances to come in, but on the fateful Saturday morning that I was scheduled to pick up my Bibles, I still had no money. One hour before I was scheduled to pick up the Bibles, I began to prepare myself for the humiliation of telling the Bible publishing company that I had no money to pay them. As I prepared to confront my embarrassment, I unexpectedly received a check for $301.25 from someone who had no knowledge that I needed $301.24 for the Bibles within the hour! It was only one penny more than the cost of the Bibles. There was absolutely no way that anyone could have known that I was in need of that exact amount of money, because I did not tell even one person. I wept with joy, knowing that Jesus was watching me so closely. The Lord wanted me to know that He was watching me and was intimately involved in my life. This was a power encounter with God in the area of my finances. It marked my heart and set me on a course of wanting to experience this more and more.

Although I have many stories that did not work out like this one, the Lord continued to encounter me in my finances throughout the next few years in very specific ways. Months after the Lord supplied for the Bibles, I gained the courage to trust Him in a specific way once again. I had continued to give my money to His kingdom beyond the 10 percent that He required. I decided to lead a junior high ski trip to Colorado over the Christmas break. Two girls in the youth group who had just become new believers really wanted to go, but they did not have the money. I committed to pay their way. I was still only making $30 a week. The price to pay for their trip was $250 a piece, or $500 total. I had believed God for $300 with the Bibles, but $500 seemed like a million dollars at the time!

I waited for the money to come for over a month, without receiving any of the $500. Even on the morning of the trip I still did not have the money. I opened the mail that day and was shocked to find a check for $250 dollars from a person who I did not know! Now, halfway to $500, we began loading the van, though I was still $250 short. Not knowing what to do, I began picturing myself washing dishes at the ski lodge to pay for the rest of their fee.

Just as we were leaving, a family friend stopped by our house and saw my van full of kids. When he saw that we were headed on a ski trip, he spontaneously gave me $250 cash! At the last hour, the Lord gave me the exact amount that I needed. Not a dollar more or less, but exactly $500. Once again Jesus wowed my heart by responding to me in a specific way in the areas of finances.

As these stories continued, I became convinced of the cause and effect dynamic that was taking place in my giving and receiving of finances. As my heart tested God in giving my money, His heart responded to me in a direct and intimate way. I became certain that God was watching me. It made my spirit vibrant. I wanted to continue by giving more and trusting His leadership to provide more. What we do with our money is one of the most practical measurements of our love for Jesus, our trust in His leadership, and our commitment to His purposes. It is important for young people to set their hearts to give extravagantly in their youth and then to maintain it over decades to build their history in God.

Developing a Personal History with God

We can determine how far we will go in God in the area of our finances. Our ability to trust Jesus' leadership increases, the amount of money He entrusts to us increases, and our joy increases through the process. We give to God and receive from Him in a supernatural way. This works together to form our personal history with God in the area of money. It affects our intimacy with Him and the amount that He will be involved in our finances. As we continue to give to and receive from Him, our personal history with God in our finances gets longer and stronger over time.

The Bible clearly describes a cause-and-effect principle in giving money to God and receiving it back from Him. God assures us that He not only sees our giving, but also responds to the very amount that we have given. Paul taught that he who sows or gives sparingly will also reap or receive sparingly, and he who *sows bountifully* will also *reap bountifully* (2 Cor. 9:10). God supernaturally multiplies the seed that we have sown. If we remain faithful to give much to God's kingdom, then God is faithful to give much back to us. Jesus said, "Give, and it will be given to you: good measure, pressed down, shaken together, and running over . . . For with the same measure that you use, it will be measured back to you" (Lk. 6:38).

The key principle is that we must *use* or give what we have before it is returned back to us in a multiplied measure. In other words, the measure of money that we give is the measure of money the Lord will give back to us.

Wherever we are at on our journey in giving, we are developing a personal, secret history with God in it. Forerunners must set their hearts to give more than 10 percent to the kingdom for the rest of their lives. No matter where we are in life, we can cultivate this personal history with God. The standards that we set in our hearts today will determine how far we go in God tomorrow. No matter what it takes, making the choice to give extravagantly now is foundational in the calling of a forerunner messenger.

The Choice of Simplicity

When I was 18 years old, I made a strong commitment to live a simple lifestyle so that I could give extravagantly to the kingdom of God. I understood that making the commitment to give extravagantly inevitably included the commitment to live a simple lifestyle. By using less money on my personal life, I could give more money to the kingdom. Paul instructed Timothy to be content with food and clothing (1 Tim. 6:8). I began to ask the Holy Spirit to show me what it meant to be content with food and clothing and other basic needs like housing and transportation. Choosing simplicity in order to give to others is very different from embracing a spirit of poverty. On the contrary, it is to live with a spirit of generosity and faith that believes God for supernatural prosperity. Kingdom simplicity is about giving, not about lacking. We do not live on less because we have less, but because we give more. We choose to live on less because we are children of a king who loves justice. Thus, we do all that we can to support works of justice in order to help others. Forerunners do not despise wealth; they want to use it to help others and thereby bring glory to God.

When I was 22 years old, my wife, Diane, and I made the commitment to live a simple lifestyle for the rest of our lives. We knew that if we neglected to give extravagantly and live simply in our twenties, it would be difficult to regain that focus in our thirties or forties. At the time, my salary at the church was $11,700 a year. We committed to double tithe.

We set our heart to give extravagantly for the rest of our lives instead of buying into the American dream of having so much more than we really needed. We did not want to fall into the common trap of subtly increasing our lifestyle comforts while decreasing the percentage of our giving. We made a commitment to decrease our lifestyle, meaning the size of our house, car, vacations, and expenses, before we would decrease the percentage of our giving to the kingdom.

When I was dating Diane before we were married, I told her the stories that I had read from the biographies of missionaries, of how God supernaturally gave finances to them. I also related each one of my personal stories of God's supernatural provision. I rehearsed in great detail how God had provided money for the Bibles, paid the way for the two girls to go on the youth ski trip, and several other stories. After we were engaged, she surprised me when she informed me that she had saved $5,000 to use after she was married. However, she was so moved by the stories that I told her that she agreed to give her $5,000 to missions. We wanted to see what God would do if we gave a large sum to His kingdom. We set our heart to begin our history together in God by giving our biggest possible gift to missions and by testing God in the area of finances. Giving $5,000 seemed like the perfect way to do this. Diane gave it all to missions. I was so proud of her.

Two years later, we bought a house through an unusual provision of the Lord. Soon after we bought it, the property zoning in our area changed from residential only to include commercial. A commercial business contacted me and asked to buy our house. We unexpectedly made $55,000 on the purchase of our home. When I brought the check to Diane, we were certain that God had returned and multiplied our $5,000 seed by putting an additional zero on the end of it! It was very clear that the $55,000 profit corresponded specifically to the $5,000 that we gave. We knew that God's eyes had been on us in this. We were so excited. It was a power encounter in the areas of finances. It wowed our hearts and made us want to give even more. Therefore, we decided to give all our new money to missions again. We wanted to see how far God would go with us when we continued to give extravagantly. He answered us again in amazing ways.

I could continue with one testimony after another of His supernatural provision in our personal family and in our ministry.

God doesn't always respond with numbers that correlate in an exact way. However, sometimes He does this so that we know without a doubt that His eye is upon us and that He is the One who is supernaturally blessing our finances. Just as the Lord has faithfully responded to us in the area of giving, so also He will surely respond when you give extravagantly.

In 1983, I had a conversation with a woman who was in need of exactly $550. She desperately needed it by the end of the day. At the time, I was making about $500 a week, which barely covered our living expenses. At the end of every month, we normally had about $100 left over. Although we did not have any extra money to give, Diane and I decided to give the woman $550, knowing that we would not have the money to pay the rent on our duplex that month unless God helped us in a supernatural way. Within two weeks, a man approached me during worship at our Tuesday night church service and whispered into my ear that God had told him to give me $550. It was the *exact amount* that we had given to the lady. I was sure that nobody knew anything about us giving the woman $550, nor did anyone know that we did not have any money to pay our rent that month. I was so excited that the Lord had provided the exact amount of money with perfect timing. I thanked the man as he put the rolled-up cash into my pocket. During the ministry time, I went to the front to pray for a couple. They told me they were in an extreme crisis and needed $550 that night. I pulled out the rolled-up cash in the exact amount of their need and handed it to them. That man's eyes grew big in amazement, wondering if I always rolled up $550 to carry around in my pocket. He began saying, "Thank you, God. Thank you, God. A miracle!"

Once again I was back to zero and unable to pay rent that month. However, I knew the Lord was watching and smiling on all of this. As I was locking up the church building that night, another man approached me on his way out. He said, "This is a bit strange, but the Lord told me to give you $550." He handed me $550. I quickly assured him that it was not strange. Twice I gave away exactly $550, and twice the Lord gave me exactly $550! He was clearly saying, "Mike, I am watching you. I am involved in your life. I want you to understand how much I care about you." I drove home from the church service that night with great joy, knowing that I had a good thing going with God. I was more determined than ever to keep this going.

By the grace of God, since that time, the Lord has met me on numerous occasions, providing supernatural finances. I get so excited each time this happens. I want all of God's people to experience power encounters in the area of their finances. These power encounters have significantly impacted my intimacy with Him. If this is new to you, know that the Lord is waiting on us to step out in faith by giving extravagantly to His kingdom as a lifestyle. He will surely meet you in His own way and in His own timing.

Unto the Fame and Purposes of God

God takes pleasure in those who trust Him by giving financially to His purposes. His eyes look to and fro across the earth for people who will trust Him enough with their money that they give extravagantly as a lifestyle. He wants to release His wealth through them. He is looking for those who will use the supernatural wealth that He gives them to finance the people, ministries, and projects that cause the fame of Jesus' name to increase in the nations.

David prayed, "God . . . bless us, and cause His face to shine upon us, that Your way may be *known on earth*, Your salvation among *all nations*" (Ps. 67:1-2). God gives us wealth so that we can promote the gospel by making the way of the Lord known in the nations.

I see a radical paradigm shift concerning money taking place in the Church in this hour. When God's servants see money, they do not envision personal increase for themselves, but they see souls being won over to Jesus, houses of prayer being financed, and acts of justice and compassion going forth to make known the fame of Jesus in the earth.

Moses said, "It is He who gives you power to get wealth, that He may establish His covenant" (Deut. 8:18). It is God who releases the power to make wealth. He does this most to those who are committed to see His covenant purposes established on the earth.

You may be a university student who only has a small amount of money. However, you must start giving extravagantly now. Giving extravagantly is not an issue of the *amount* of money that you give but of the *percentage* of your income that you give. This is the time for you to set your heart to support the prayer and missions movement that is growing so fast in the earth at this time. God can easily release wealth to you in a short amount of time.

I strongly encourage all believers to give regularly to the kingdom of God. Some years ago, I spoke to a lady who was a new believer in the church that I pastored. She was in desperate need of $2,000 by 5:00pm that day. I told her that I wanted to help her. However, I wanted to first talk to her about tithing as the first step in having God's order and blessing in her finances. She instantly said that she could *not afford to tithe*. I shared from the Scriptures and gave her a few personal testimonies. I assured her that *she could not afford not to tithe* because she needed

God's supernatural involvement in her finances. After receiving my exhortation from the Scripture on giving, she made a commitment to the Lord to start tithing. I told her that if she was willing to trust God in her finances, I would join her by committing to personally help her get the $2,000. I was determined not to present her need to the church's compassion fund. I wanted to see what the Lord would do, if we both set our hearts to look to Him to meet her need.

I definitely did not have $2,000, so we needed a miracle by 5:00pm that day. It was still before noon. So, we had over five hours for a miracle of finance to take place. Soon after my conversation with this woman, a young couple I did not know came to my church office and asked me to pray for them. The husband was having regular nightmares and was under a deep sense of oppression. He had heard that our church prayed for the sick. When I laid hands on him and prayed a simple prayer, the man began coughing and choking as a demon was manifesting. His wife was a bit concerned as she witnessed her husband choking and contorting in a strange way. After a short time of prayer, he was totally delivered and filled with joy. His countenance was completely different. He was so happy. Spontaneously, he pulled out his checkbook and wrote a check for $2,000. He left the name blank and told me that I could write it to anyone. I assured him that he did not need to do that, but he insisted. They both left my office rejoicing.

I was holding the $2,000 in my hand—the money that I had committed to give to the lady I had just spoken with. God supplied me with the exact amount of money that she needed in the exact time that she needed it! This really touched me. It was another financial miracle or power encounter in my history in God. The lady was also overjoyed, having witnessed her first financial power encounter. She was committed to start a life of faith and obedience in the area of her finances.

A few months after this, the story was repeated. This time a single mom from our church asked me for help. She desperately needed a car so that she could drive to work. She was very close to losing her job. I committed to help her. However, I wanted to first talk to her about tithing. She also said that she could *not afford to tithe*. I again shared from the Scriptures and gave her a few personal testimonies. I assured her that *she could not afford not to tithe* because she needed God's supernatural involvement in her finances. She only made $150 a week and could not afford to give even $15 away. I told her that God was calling her to a new dimension of her relationship with Jesus, by trusting Him to provide for her as she faithfully gave her tithes. She made a commitment to the Lord to start tithing. I told her that if she was willing to trust God in her finances, then I would join her by committing to personally help get her a car. I felt the Lord was going to help us, if we both set our hearts to look to Him to supply a car. We committed to tell no one about this need. We wanted to see what the Lord would do.

That very night, at our church service, a very unusual thing happened. A man handed me a blank title deed for a car. He said, "This is odd, but the Lord told me to give this to you and to put whoever's name on the deed that you wish!" I have never had that happen before or since. I called the woman that night and asked her if she was still committed to tithing her money to God. She said she did not know how she would afford it, but, yes, she was committed no matter what. I then told her about the title deed. She was overjoyed. She could hardly believe it. God supplied me with a car at the exact time that this single mom needed it! This really touched me. This lady also made a commitment to the Lord to trust and obey Him with her finances.

Refusing to Give That which Costs Us Nothing

Part of the commitment of the Sacred Charge is to set our heart to give extravagantly to God's kingdom purposes in world missions, helping the oppressed, and so on.

However, there is something more, in addition to winning the lost and helping the needy. There is a further dimension to extravagant giving. We also give because it is a way to express Jesus' worthiness and our love for Him.

I love the story in David's life when he refused to give God an offering that cost him nothing. When David attempted to purchase a plot of land on which to build an altar and give an offering to the Lord, the owner of the land offered to give the property to King David as a free gift. Out of an expression of love for God, David rejected the offer by insisting on buying the land, because he would not offer to the LORD that which cost him nothing (2 Sam. 24:24).

God is moved when we live in a way that costs us something as we express our love to Jesus. The way that we give money should express our trust in God's leadership over our finances, our commitment to the harvest, and our dedication to works of justice. However, there is more. We must give in ways that directly express love. This is not an issue of how much money we give; it is an issue of the percentage of our money that we give. Jesus made this point famously when he compared the giving of a widow with the giving of the rich. He said the "poor widow has put in more than all; for all these *out of their abundance* have put in offerings for God, but she *out of her poverty put in all the livelihood* that she had" (Lk. 21:3-4).

We only give extravagantly when we give that which costs

us. The rich gave more money than the poor widow, but the widow gave a greater percentage of her income than the rich. She really felt the effects of her giving. Jesus pointed her out as an example of actually giving *more* from God's point of view. We, too, must set our hearts to refuse to give that which costs us nothing and barely affects our personal lives. We want to give in a way that clearly expresses our love for Jesus.

As forerunners, let us take on God's challenge to give in a way that costs us and moves God's heart because of our love. In the early days of our walk with Jesus, we must set our heart in the matter of giving. Ask the Lord how much of your income is for you to keep for your personal needs and how much is for you to give away to build the kingdom.

I have set my heart to give my money to people and ministries that focus on equipping people to walk in wholehearted obedience to Jesus, consistent prayer, and to operate in the power of the Spirit as they seek to reach the lost, help the poor and oppressed, and heal the sick.

Make a commitment to give a specific percent of your income and never go back on it. Once He allows you to give twenty percent, push to thirty, then forty percent. *Set your heart to decrease your lifestyle before you decrease the percent of your giving.* Choose to live simply. Extravagant giving builds our relationship with Jesus and it builds the kingdom by helping others. In giving, our love for Jesus grows, as does our love for others, as our heart is wowed over and over again. What an amazing way to live.

CHAPTER 7

Live Holy

Living Fascinated in the Pleasures of Loving God

The Lord calls us to holiness because He is holy. We only experience the joy of walking with Him as we walk in holiness. Though many see holiness as the drudgery of self-denial, the truth is that His holiness is the most pleasurable and exhilarating quality of life in existence. It is how God lives. He wants to share His life with us, that we may enjoy this superior quality of life in the liberty of holiness. We are called to live fascinated in the pleasure of loving God that overflows in loving people. It is far from a life of drudgery—it is living with a heart that is vibrant in love for Jesus and people.

In truth, holiness equips us to enjoy life together with God forever. The Lord declares, "Be holy, for I am holy" (1 Pet. 1:16). We must not approach holiness with a sense of dread and fear of boredom. Holiness does not keep us from pleasure; it equips us to experience the pleasure of living wholeheartedly in God. The power of holiness sets us free from the vain imaginations, defilement, and dullness of lust, pride, and bitterness.

In our pursuit to live holy, I want to consider two foundational truths. The first is that we must be preoccupied with the superior pleasures of God. The second truth is that out of this preoccupation with the pleasures of knowing God, we must set our hearts on hundredfold obedience. Comprehending and embracing these two truths will provide the foundation for living holy in the midst of a wicked and perverse generation.

Foundational Truth #1: Being Preoccupied with Superior Pleasures

God has created every human being with a longing for pleasure and a longing to be fascinated. Though this may seem obvious, for some people this is a new idea. Unfortunately, there is a prevalent, but untrue, sentiment in the Body of Christ that pleasure is wrong and usually only associated with sinful desires. The truth is that God is the author of pleasure and, as such, He has created us to enjoy physical, mental, emotional, and spiritual pleasures. For all eternity, we will experience all of these pleasures in heaven. However, the greatest of all the pleasures that are available to the human spirit are spiritual pleasures that come when God reveals God to the human spirit—that is, when God, the Holy Spirit, reveals God, the Father and the Son, to our heart.

Our longing for pleasure is part of the design that God specifically created us with. Therefore, it must be satisfied. Our longing for pleasure will never, ever go away. For all eternity, we will have longings for pleasure. The good news is that we will be infinitely and eternally satisfied in our resurrected bodies, living in God's immediate presence.

Satan tempts us with fleeting and counterfeit pleasures. He does this to distract us from the superior pleasures of encountering God. He seeks to allure us with physical and emotional pleasures that are outside God's will. They cannot ever satisfy the deep longing for pleasure that is in our spirit. They actually keep us from experiencing the higher, more exhilarating pleasures of encountering God that are available to all of us through a relationship with Jesus.

The truest and greatest pleasures available to the human spirit do not come from the counterfeit pleasures of sin, but come from God when He reveals Himself to our spirits. The revelation and experience of God exhilarates our spirit at the deepest levels. The tragedy of giving way to the temporary "pleasures" of sin is that it cheats us of experiencing the higher pleasures by settling for the lesser. We are liberated from the inferior pleasures of sin by experiencing these superior pleasures of the love, beauty, and majesty of Jesus.

As believers, we have the greatest and most gratifying pleasures available to us from God. Paul taught that the Holy Spirit *searches* all things, even *the deep things* of God's heart. We have received the Spirit that we might *know the things* that have been freely given to us by God (1 Cor. 2:10-12).

The Holy Spirit searches, or discerns, the "deep things" of the Father's heart and mind, including the delight He feels for Jesus, the saints, and His kingdom. The Spirit helps us to feel some of what the Father feels. The Spirit escorts us on what I refer to as the holy "treasure hunt" into the knowledge and beauty of Jesus.

Jesus promised us that the Holy Spirit would glorify Jesus in us by taking the things that belong to Jesus and making them known to us (Jn. 16:14-15). The Holy Spirit takes the things that Jesus is thinking and feeling and reveals them to us. This is divine "entertainment" at its highest. The Lord releases small measures of insight and inspiration from the Word to our heart. They tenderize our spirits for a few moments. These subtle flashes of glory upon our hearts are to be a regular part of our relationship with God. Over time, this holy influence changes our lives, causing us to live holy.

In comparing sin with the experience of God, C. S. Lewis wrote this staggering statement:

> If we consider the unblushing promises of reward and the staggering nature of the rewards promised in the Gospels, it would seem that *Our Lord finds our desires, not too strong, but too weak.* We are half-hearted creatures, fooling about with drink and sex and ambition when infinite joy is offered us, like an ignorant child who wants to go on making mud pies in a slum because he cannot imagine what is meant by the offer of a holiday at the sea. *We are far too easily pleased.*
>
> —C. S. Lewis, *The Weight of Glory*

Many of the approaches to pursuing holiness have placed the emphasis of holy living on self-denial rather than fascination with God. It is biblical to call people to deny themselves of sinful lusts and pleasures. However, the best way to overcome darkness is not by focusing on the darkness of sin and trying to do our best to resist sin. The most practical and successful way to resist sin is to focus on "the light of the knowledge of the glory of God in the face of Jesus Christ" (2 Cor. 4:6) rather than the darkness of lust. No one seeks to remove darkness in a room by opening a window to throw out buckets full of darkness. The best way to remove darkness from a room is to simply turn on the light. We will not overcome the darkness of immorality, bitterness, and pride by focusing on it. We do not decrease the darkness in us by focusing on darkness. The way for darkness to decrease in us is to for us to focus on increasing the amount of light we receive and enjoy. We overcome sin by actively encountering more of Jesus, not simply by resisting sin.

One of King David's lifelong goals was to encounter the beauty of God on a regular basis. As the king of Israel, David maintained many responsibilities, including weighty responsibilities of leading Israel's government and military as the king. Yet his supreme desire, as king and head of the army, was to behold the beauty of God. David unashamedly declared, "One thing I have desired . . . all the days of my life, to behold the beauty of the Lord" (Ps. 27:4). His heart was not distracted by lesser things, but was preoccupied with a vision to encounter God. In other words, we do not need to disconnect from everything in life in order to make this preoccupation real. David continued as king of Israel. David knew that the way to best love God and to be exhilarated by God was to take time to gaze on Him, or to be in His presence.

David said, "In your presence is fullness of joy; at your right hand are pleasures forevermore" (Ps. 16:11). In other words, the nearer somebody gets to God, the more joy that person will encounter, because God is the fullness of joy. God's throne is the epicenter of joy in the universe, and those nearest His throne enjoy the greatest measure of joy available. God is a happy God with a happy heart. He is the very fountain of joy.

David prayed to drink from the river of His pleasures (Ps. 36:8). We do this as the Holy Spirit reveals the beauty of God to our spirit. In the generation of the Lord's return, experiencing the superior pleasures of Jesus' beauty will be emphasized by the Spirit. Isaiah prophesied that in that day (the last days) the Branch of the Lord (Jesus the Messiah) would be seen as beautiful and glorious (Isa. 4:2). We are approaching a time frame in history when the worldwide Body of Christ will experience an unusual amount of revelation concerning the deep things of God's heart. There will be great revelation of the beauty of Jesus. As we approach the end of the age, living fascinated by the beauty and glory of Jesus is an essential component of maintaining fervent love for Jesus. Loving Jesus is the fountain and wellspring of happy holiness.

Our Longing to Be Fascinated

Like our longing to experience pleasure, God has created in us a deep desire to be fascinated. We love to be awestruck. We love to marvel and be filled with wonder. This capacity to be fascinated was carefully crafted into our spirits by the genius of God when He created us. This longing must be satisfied. It will not remain neutral and it will not simply go away over time. This longing to be fascinated will either be satisfied the right way in God, or the wrong way by darkness.

The secular entertainment industry has identified and targeted this God-ordained longing in the human spirit. They have exploited this God-initiated craving to their profit and our ruin. Entertainment has become one of the primary felt needs in the Western world. The priority of the minds of many people is to achieve a lifestyle where they can secure more and more entertainment.

We cannot repent of our longing to be fascinated. It is God-given. It was built into our design when God created us as recorded in Genesis chapter 1. However, we will only satisfy this longing to be fascinated when we are fascinated by the revelation of Jesus. The apostle Paul was preoccupied with being fascinated by the knowledge of Jesus. It was the key to his vision for his life, as seen in his self-revealing confession: "I also count all things loss for *the excellence of the knowledge of Christ*" (Phil. 3:8).

Without a sense of marvel with God, in which our spirit connects with Jesus in new ways, we will live spiritually bored. A spiritually bored believer is far more vulnerable to the enemy's temptations. If we do not answer the longing for fascination in the right way by encountering Jesus more and more, then we will seek to answer this longing in the wrong way. Living with a sense of awe in our relationship with God empowers our inner man. It causes us to live with fascination and a deep sense of purpose. This is what best equips us to resist temptation. The enemy's attempts to distract us with lesser temptations are thwarted in us as we grow in deep revelation of Jesus. Those whose lives are fascinated with Jesus overcome temptation with far greater success. There is great power in being preoccupied with fascination with Jesus.

Moses chose "rather to suffer affliction with the people of God than to enjoy the passing pleasures of sin" (Heb. 11:25). Moses knew that sin had pleasure for a brief moment. He knew it was a momentary and passing pleasure. He also knew it was no real contest when compared to the pleasures of God. The reason we choose sin is because we believe the lie that its pleasures are superior to the pleasure of connecting with God. The entertainment industry thrives on this illusion, and many fall for fascinations far lesser than knowing the One who created the heavens and earth and who loves us with everlasting love (Jer. 31:3). The Maker, who wraps himself in light and sits above the circle of the earth, is so fascinating that no eye has yet seen, no ear has heard, and no mind has ever imagined the depths of His glory (Ps. 104:2; 1 Cor. 2:9). The pleasure of sin is only for a moment, for minutes, yet the fascinating glories of God are for-ever. There is far more satisfaction in connecting with God than any other thing.

God will fill our desire for fascination and pleasure forev-er, not just in the next age, but He will touch us and satisfy us even now in a substantial way. However, we know that we will not know perfect satisfaction until we see Him face to face (Ps. 17:15; 1 Jn. 3:1-3). Holiness is not just a good idea for the dis-tant future. It is possible to live with a holy preoccupation in be-ing fascinated with the beauty of Jesus today. Every believer is weak and broken; yet it is the power of the Spirit who enables us receive revelation of the Father and the Son (Eph. 1:17-19). The battle for holiness is the battle to become preoccupied through fascination and to experience the wealth of pleasures found in a heart that is alive with the love of God.

Foundational Truth #2: Setting our Hearts on Hundredfold Obedience

As our soul awakens to the holy love of God through spiri-tual pleasure and fascination, we are empowered to set our heart to love and obey God with all our heart. Jesus said, "If you love Me, keep My commandments" (Jn. 14:15). Part of God's gift to our heart is our very love and desire for Him. The God who calls for our full dedication to Him, it the very One who empowers us to give it. When we set our hearts to live in 100 percent obedi-ence, our emotions are significantly impacted and our heart is spiritually vibrant.

When we establish our commitment to live in hundredfold obedience, we experience a dynamic spark in our relationship with God that we would otherwise never have known. There is a deep encounter between God and our spirit that is experienced on a consistent basis, only when every area of life seeks to be yielded to God. There is a measure of blessing released upon the human spirit, only when our *heart is set* to live in 100 percent obedience to God. Holding back even one issue from the leadership of the Spirit affects our emotional make-up and hinders our ability to experience God fully. I have found that 98 percent obedience has a limited blessing. The last 2 percent positions our heart to receive the joy of God's spirit, igniting vibrancy in our inner man. There is a "spark" of the Spirit in our hearts as we reach out to Him and aim to live this way. We must not settle for 98 percent, but live with a vision for complete obedience and the fullness of encounter.

Aiming for hundredfold obedience includes bridling our speech (Jas. 3:2), making a covenant with our eyes that refuses to look on anything that stirs up lust (Job 31:1), disciplining our physical appetites, managing our time to give ourselves more fully to prayer and works of the kingdom, and stewarding our money to advance His kingdom. There is a big difference between attaining 100 percent obedience and aiming or reaching for it. His blessings are not released after we *reach* holiness, but when we *set our heart* to fully aim for it. When we intentionally "reach" in our spirit to obey Jesus in literally every area of our life—our speech, eyes, time, money, etc.—we experience a new dimension in the grace of God. I am referring to more than a casual commitment to obey God in a general way. I am referring to a specific goal to fully obey Him in every area of our life. The very reach of our heart to live this way has a dynamic impact on our emotions.

The Lord values our journey to grow in love and fully enjoys us as we mature in Him. When we sin, we repent with the knowledge of God's love over our lives and we renew our resolve to fully love Him in every area of lives. Even in our weakness, God honors the position of our heart, as we desire to fully love Him. The attitude and desire of the heart is what He sees and what He blesses with fresh experiences of His grace.

When we set our heart to love and obey God fully, the Spirit strengthens us. The psalmist taught, "Because he has set his love upon Me, therefore I will deliver him" (Ps. 91:14). Obedience and love start as a choice. God has given the human race great dignity in giving us a free will with the ability to make choices to love that will last forever.

We must not underestimate the power of our choices. The Holy Spirit honors the power of our decisions. We have the ability to set our affections on anything that we choose. When we make the heart choice to set our love upon God, we put ourselves in the path of the Holy Spirit, and He responds to us. Our decisions by themselves are not enough to change our emotions, yet they play an important role in the process of our transformation. As we change our mind, the Spirit changes our heart and brings our emotions under His leadership. When we make the choice to love Him fully, the Spirit helps our heart feel His love and love Him in return.

God created us with a deep longing for our love to be wholehearted and we cannot function properly until we have set our hearts to be fully His. Many seek security and fulfillment in God without being abandoned to Him. Halfhearted followers of God most often struggle with a sense of emptiness, burnout, boredom, and discontentment *because they have too much of God to enjoy sin and too much sin to enjoy God*. Living short of 100 percent obedience to God actually diminishes our glory as human beings. Living in wholehearted abandon to God is God's gift to us. It is His invitation to us to experience the fullness of glory that He intended for the human race.

The passionate God created us with the need to be passionate. We were created for the glory of love and we soar to the heights of our human potential only when we set our heart to fully love God. There is nothing more satisfying than to know we are giving our all to God. God doesn't require wholeheartedness because of an insufficiency in Him. Rather, God knows that only in fully loving Him are we able to experience the fullness of what it means to be human. God is entirely self-sufficient, yet He desires our love. He does not need us, yet He abounds in desire for us. As we express our desire for Him in our daily actions, we soar in the joy of love. Setting our heart to fully obey and love always enables us to function at our highest potential.

Three Practical Principles of Holy Living

There is a divine exchange between humans and God in the pursuit of holy abandonment. God requires us to play a part by cooperating with Him in the grace of God instead of receiving His grace in vain. The Bible describes a division of labor where God releases grace and we choose to cooperate with the grace He gives. Paul expressed this when he said, "We then . . . plead with you not to receive the grace of God in vain" (2 Cor. 6:1). God will be faithful to release grace upon us, but we must choose to fully embrace His grace in the daily choices of our lives.

God will not do our part and we cannot do God's part in the divine cooperation of a holy lifestyle. Our part includes making quality decisions to deny ourselves the lesser and temporary pleasures of sin, feeding our spirits on the Word, asking for His help through prayer, pursuing godly activities, and embracing only godly relationships. God's part includes releasing supernatural influences upon our heart (new godly desires), on our body (healing), on our circumstances (provision and protection), on our relationships (favor), and in our ministry.

We must dialogue with God about the issues of our lives and submit our resources to His leadership every day. When we cooperate in the grace of God in this way, God will honor His part to release the supernatural influences of power, wisdom, and desires upon our heart, bring healing to our physical bodies, release provision and protection on our circumstances, favor on our relationships, and blessing on our ministry. God will not do our job, but He will help us if we choose to receive His divine assistance. We must be in cooperation with Him and His grace in order to experience the life we desire.

In order to experience the foundational truths of experiencing pleasure and living in 100 percent obedience, there are three practical principles outlined in Scripture that help us attain the goal of holiness. Paul outlines these principles in order to help the Church to practically understand holiness:

> Reckon yourselves to be dead indeed to sin, but alive to God in Christ Jesus our Lord. Therefore do not let sin reign in your mortal body, that you should obey it in its lusts. And do not present your members as instruments of unrighteousness to sin, but present yourselves to God as being alive from the dead, and your members as instruments of righteousness to God.
>
> —Romans 6:11-13

In this passage, I have identified three principles: the *knowing* principle (Rom. 6:11), the *resisting* principle (Rom. 6:12-13a), and the *pursuing* principle (Rom. 6:13b). We must know truth, resist darkness, and pursue God. All three are vital to maintaining a life in godliness and cannot be exchanged for another. In each point, it is vital that we cooperate with the grace that God gives us in order to fully embrace the call of holiness.

These three practical principles described by Paul specifically reveal our role in agreeing with and acting on the grace of God. Paul describes the knowing principle, saying, *"Reckon [or see] yourselves* to be dead indeed to sin, but alive to God in Christ"* (Rom. 6:11). In order to resist sin and pursue God in a right way, there are certain truths that we need to *know* and understand. We must know who we are in Christ, what He did for us, and what we receive in Him. We all received the gift of righteousness, the indwelling Spirit, and authority to use the name of Jesus. We are to reckon, or see, ourselves as dead to sin and alive to God because of the finished work of Jesus on the cross and His resurrection from the dead. We must understand the truth about God's heart, that He is our Father and our Bridegroom. As we grow in knowledge concerning the good things which are in us in Christ Jesus, our faith becomes effective (Philemon 6). In order to effectively resist sin, we must gain understanding concerning our faith.

The resisting principle is described thus: *"Do not let sin reign* in your mortal body, that you should obey it in its lusts. And *do not present your members* as instruments of unrighteousness to sin"* (Rom. 6:12-13). We must resist Satan, sin, and sin-provoking circumstances in order to live holy lives before God. It is not enough to know who we are; we must put knowledge into action by resisting inferior pleasures and embracing increased knowledge concerning God. We must not go to places, buy items, look at, or talk about that which stirs up our sinful passions. We must agree with the grace of God to actively resist anything that would hinder our love for Him.

Paul presents the pursuing principle, saying, *"Present your-selves* to God as being alive from the dead, and *your members* as instruments of righteousness"* (Rom. 6:13). We must actively pursue intimacy with God and present our bodies as instruments that He can use to bless others as we serve them and release the power and presence of Jesus in their lives. We pursue serving with humility, ministering to people in the power of the Holy Spirit and relating to God and people with love. In pursuing lives of holiness, it is vital that we live out the first and second great commandments by actively pursuing God every day and being vessels of love and power towards others.

All three of these principles must operate together in our lives. It is not enough to just resist sin and pursue God, without knowing who we are in Christ. Likewise, it is not enough to pursue God at prayer meetings without resisting sin. It does not work to only know truth and to resist sin without actively pursuing love for God and for people.

Living Holy: It Is Possible

A life of holiness in which we love God in every area of our life is possible now. It is not for the super-Christian, it is not for the future when we are fully mature, and it is not waiting for us only on the other side of eternity. It begins today—step by step, choice by choice, yes by yes. We must choose to love God with all that we are, one moment at a time, because He loved us with all that He had. He loved us to the end. Let us find ourselves fascinated by Him, experiencing the supreme spiritual pleasure of His love, and living in 100 percent obedience to His ways. Let us live holy, loving the Lord our God with all of our heart, all of our mind, and all of our strength.

CHAPTER 8

Lead Diligently

Taking Initiative to Minister to Others

S imply put, a leader is someone who other people follow. If people are not following us, then we are not yet a leader. It does not matter what our leadership title or position is or is not. When people voluntarily follow us by doing what we do, then we are a leader. When others seek to imitate our faith, then we are a leader. It does not matter how many people are following us. Some will lead hundreds, others may lead thousands, and some will only lead individuals. It does not matter how many we lead; what matters is *where* we lead and *how* we lead them. We must lead to Jesus instead of to ourselves and we must take the initiative to lead with diligence, without passivity and slothfulness.

Leadership is hard work; it requires taking initiative. Do not wait to be asked before you give yourself to do the hard tasks that others do not want to do. There is a great need for any who will take initiative to lead in outreaches, prayer meetings, home groups, Bible studies, or in making disciples of younger believers.

Jesus declared, "All authority has been given to Me in heaven and on earth. Go therefore and *make disciples* of all the nations

. . . *teaching them* to observe all things that I have commanded you" (Mt. 28:18-20). The call to servant leadership is a call to make disciples. This calling is so important that Jesus included it in His final message to His disciples after His resurrection. The call to make disciples has many diverse and creative expressions. We are called to disciple both individuals and nations.

Discipling individuals can occur in one-on-one meetings or in small group settings. Jesus made disciples in a small-group setting. It takes time, effort, and commitment to do this consistently in a one-on-one meeting or in small groups meetings. However, the impact we make by doing this is very rewarding and long-lasting.

We disciple nations by impacting various areas of society with God's Word and presence. In this way, we engage with the culture by being salt and light. Leaders like Bill Bright of Campus Crusade for Christ and Loren Cunningham of Youth With A Mission have identified the seven most important spheres of society that Christians are to impact in order to disciple nations. These seven spheres are:

1. Family

2. Education

3. Government (politics, law, and the military)

4. Economy (business, science, and technology)

5. Arts (entertainment and sports)

6. Media

7. Religion

God has placed His people in each sphere. Jesus has called us to bring His Word and presence to impact all seven of these spheres.

God has a plan to win your campus or city. We are to ask Him what role we are to play in serving His plan in our campus or city. He will give specific assignments and creative ideas of how to reach people when we simply ask for them. Ask God where your harvest field is. Is it in your campus, neighborhood, marketplace, or a foreign land? As He progressively reveals His plan to you, follow Him in the small steps that He puts before you. They will inevitably add up and lead to the fulfillment of His greater purposes in your life, and the lives of those around you.

In moving forward in leadership, ask what practical things need to be done in the ministry organization that you are in and ask yourself what you want to do. Serve in practical ways, showing yourself faithful, and the Lord will increase your portion in a future season.

Help start and lead prayer meetings and outreaches on your campus, in the marketplace, or in your neighborhood. Lead weekly Bible studies or discussion groups that allow you to disciple younger believers. Whether we are in vocational ministry, the marketplace, in school, or at home, we have been strategically placed there to provide leadership to others. It doesn't need to be over a multitude of people—we may just impact one or two people at a time.

The question is not who is most qualified or the most gifted, but who will take the initiative to invest in others to help them understand and connect more with Jesus.

Leadership is about investing in people. It does not require a certain personality type, ministry position, or title. Most leadership does not happen from a platform with a microphone but in small-group or one-on-one settings. God is looking for an army of men and women who will take on the challenge of discipling younger believers.

Leading with Diligence

Paul exhorted the saints to use the spiritual gifts, such as prophecy, teaching, leadership, and giving (Rom. 12:6-8). When Paul mentioned leadership, he emphasized that those who lead should do so "with diligence" (Rom. 12:8). Although diligence is not the only issue in leadership, it is a critical component of leadership and is most commonly neglected. Diligence in leadership is a rare but very valuable quality.

Diligence, as defined by one dictionary, is "the constant and earnest effort to accomplish what is undertaken with persistent exertion." We must recognize that leadership is not halfhearted, but is earnest in its efforts. It is not by definition something that is done on a short-term basis. A diligent leader is one who takes initiative in a long-term way. It lasts for more than one summer or one semester of school, or even one year.

Leading with diligence includes zealously investing our energy to develop our God-given skills over a long period of time. It is what we do outside of our job or ministry to develop our skill. It impacts the way we spend our money, personal time, and energy so that we can fulfill our assignment before God in the most complete way.

Some people have skill because of natural gifting, but they lack diligence in using their God-given skills. Thus, they will never reach the fullness of God's plan for their life. Solomon wisely stated: "He who has a slack hand becomes poor, but the hand of the diligent makes rich" (Prov. 10:4). The slack person in the proverb did not start off poor, but became poor because they were not earnest with their gift over time. Consequently, they lost what they formerly had. On the contrary, the diligent became rich and entered into the fullness of what God had destined for them. Our goal is to enter into the fullness of what God has given to us.

Moreover, Solomon tells us that "the hand of the diligent will rule, but the lazy man will be put to forced labor . . . diligence is man's precious possession" (Prov. 12:24, 27). Many obtain a position in ministry or influence because of their God-given gifting, but then lose it over time because they lack diligence in the use of their gifts. While some skills and talents are given as a gift from God from birth, diligence is man's precious possession that is acquired over time. Diligence is the means by which our God-given skill moves into its fullness.

Twelve Characteristics of a Diligent Leader

There are many characteristics that contribute to having greater effectiveness in leadership. I identified a few that are very important for any who seek to lead effectively.

Leadership Characteristic #1: Have a Clear Vision or a Deep Sense of Purpose

One of the most important keys to effective leadership is having a clear vision or a deep sense of purpose. In order to efficiently lead others you must be a man or woman of purpose—a purpose that is so strong that you refuse to be denied of it. Some leaders are aimless; they lack clear goals and are not sure what they are aiming for. Therefore, they are not able to call others to join them in their goals. Leaders should be able to tell others clearly what they want and where they are going. They must have a clear picture of what they want now and what they want to accomplish over the next ten years, or even the next forty years. They do not have to know all the specific application or details, but should have clarity about the general direction in which they want to build their ministry. They should be able to describe it to others at least in a general way.

For example, I was clear that one day I was going to lead a ministry of missionaries that would be mobilized in 24/7 prayer and worship. I had that vision for sixteen years *before* I began the IHOP–KC Missions Base. I did not have all the details or the specific application, but I knew the general direction of where I wanted to go.

Effective leaders diligently pursue their vision. It is a personal and spiritual issue between them and God. When leaders possess a sense of having an assignment from heaven, they become serious about their calling. We need to ask ourselves the question: what do I refuse to be denied? When there is a resolve within your heart to not be denied something that God has called you to, doors will eventually open in God's timing.

The Lord told the prophet Habakkuk to *write the vision* and make it plain on tablets so that the people who read it might run with the vision (Hab. 2:2). We should clearly write out our vision, along with a simple action plan that describes how we plan to pursue it. This means talking with God until you have specific goals that you desire to accomplish over the next twelve months, ten years, or forty years. Break it down practically and write it out. This way you will make the invisible visible for others to see and follow. Without an action plan with clear goals to aim for, most will walk aimlessly, being unable to accomplish their vision. Because multi-talented people can do many things, obtaining a clear vision and an action plan helps leaders focus in order to meet their goals in a practical way.

Leadership Characteristic #2: Taking the Initiative to Act

A second characteristic of diligent leadership is taking the initiative to act. Simply put, leaders must take action. They must work hard to succeed. Solomon expresses it in this way:

"The . . . lazy man *desires*, and has nothing; but the . . . *diligent* shall be made *rich*" (Prov. 13:4). The dreamer may dream of leadership, but he stops at desire and does not move on to action. The diligent take initiative to act on their vision.

A healthy leadership culture is one that emphasizes taking initiative. Real leaders take initiative. They are not waiting to be asked or "discovered" as they sit idly in the congregation. It is a common misconception within the Church that taking initiative is synonymous with pride and self-promotion. Promoting oneself is more about demanding a position of honor. Leaders who take initiative operate with a different spirit from those who demand a position of honor.

Many live in frustration for years, idly waiting to be asked to serve in a ministry. Rather than waiting to be asked, it is far better to start doing what needs to be done. Taking initiative to reach out in ministry to people requires humility and vulnerability in taking a risk of failure. The sign of a good leader is one who will take responsibility to start or strengthen a ministry without waiting to be asked. They do not blame others for not being given an opportunity lead, or if their new ministry does not succeed.

At IHOP–KC we expect those with a call to leadership to take initiative to minister to people without waiting to be recruited. I learned this from the youth group that I was in over thirty years ago. When I was in high school, my youth leaders encouraged me to begin a Bible study at the junior high school with believers who were younger than me.

While I was at university, my youth leaders again urged me to take initiative to start a Bible study there just like I did when I was in high school. I photocopied one thousand flyers and passed them out to students walking around the campus, inviting them to come to my Thursday night Bible study. Although I knew very few people on campus, my Bible study grew from thirty to two hundred students in one year!

I refused to be denied what was in my heart. I had a vision to start a campus ministry, so I took the initiative to start one. Since I believed that I was called to teach the Bible, I took the initiative to develop my calling to teach the Bible. I did not wait for somebody to give me an opportunity to speak in a Bible study that already existed.

Over my years of pastoring, I have always looked for those young men and women who have the diligence, courage, and initiative to start a ministry or to serve in an existing one, instead of waiting to be asked. Today is the perfect time to develop your leadership skills by taking the initiative and serving those around you. Ask the Holy Spirit for direction concerning whom to reach out to in your church or city, then just start reaching out to them. Don't wait for a leader to ask you to do it; just do it!

Leadership Characteristic #3: Leaders Take Risks

Risk-taking is a vital characteristic of leadership. Too many potential leaders wait until a ministry is successful before they commit to it. Take a risk and step out to move forward in ministry. Ask the Holy Spirit to give you a nudge as to which direction to start investing time and energy into, and then just start. Do not worry about failure. Remember, no one can steer a parked car. The Holy Spirit cannot steer your ministry if it is "parked," so launch out and begin reaching out to believers and unbelievers alike.

Throughout the years, I have started a number of ministries that ended up fizzling out. It is not a big deal that some have not worked. I feel the Lord's pleasure in the fact that I am trying new ways to reach out to help people know and love Him. The successful ministries that I have done would never have gotten off the ground unless I had been willing to take a risk and even risk failure.

Although leaders face fear like every other person, they should not driven by fear, but by the vision that is in their heart. Jesus taught His disciples this principle through the parable of the talents: "He who had received the *one talent* . . . said, 'Lord, I knew you to be a hard man, reaping where you have not sown . . . I was *afraid,* and went and *hid* your talent in the ground.' But his Lord answered and said to him, 'You *wicked* and *lazy* servant . . .'" (Mt. 25:24-28). Many hide their fear and laziness behind spiritual excuses, but real leaders take risks by pushing past their fear and using even the small talent that God has given them. Every one of us should engage in some practical way to reach out to people.

Some can seek to help lead a prayer meeting or Bible study, or gather a few younger believers in a small group to start discipling them, or pray for the sick, or reach out to those who are lost or who have a specific need. We can make a difference even in small ways. We must not wait passively for someone to ask us, or for our long-term goals to suddenly come to pass. We should take risks by putting our hand to something practical now. The very act of reaching out in these ways will also be used by God to help you develop your ministry gifts and callings.

Leadership Characteristic #4: Being Faithful in Times of Smallness

Being faithful in small things is an important characteristic of a leader. Some are waiting for a larger position of platform ministry to open up to them before they begin to serve. Being faithful and diligent when your ministry is small is a very important part of being a true leader. Anyone can be diligent when they are in the limelight of many people receiving their ministry. Jesus will say, "Well done," to those who are faithful over a few things, as He makes them a ruler over many" (Mt. 25:21). It is so important that we are diligent in assignments that are small and that go unnoticed by others. We can trust Him to entrust a greater sphere of responsibility to us in His own timing.

I first received the vision for 24/7 prayer and worship in May 1983. We did not start IHOP–KC for another sixteen years. I led really small prayer meetings on an almost daily basis for the entire sixteen years before IHOP–KC started in May 1999.

Over the years, I have had many share with me their desire to start a 24/7 prayer room in their city. The questions they usually ask me are about how to structure the meetings, how to get a building, or who can help them build a website, and what sort of marketing strategy they should use. I always tell them that buildings, websites, and structures are the easy part. The most challenging part is to find people who will help them faithfully lead small prayer meetings day after day, month after month, year after year. The Lord may ask you to be faithful and diligent with smallness for years.

We can remain diligent and faithful as we live before an audience of One, before God's eyes alone. Some people only serve with diligence when other leaders are watching. It is common to see people leading diligently in ministry when they are seeking to be noticed so that they may gain approval from their leaders. However, these same people are passive and lazy once they gain the ministry position they were after. Such people usually end up losing the position of honor over time due to a lack of diligence.

Paul promises, "Whatever you do, do it heartily, as to the Lord and not to men, knowing that from the Lord you will receive the reward of the inheritance; for you serve the Lord Christ" (Col. 3:23-24). Many are willing to serve with diligence when their leaders are watching, but real leaders are zealous and diligent to go the extra mile when no one sees. Work hard for God and His reward, not so that you will be noticed and rewarded by men or so that you will obtain a leadership position now. When we work for God first, our hearts feel more joy and more gratification as He touches us and empowers us to be faithful and enthusiastic in secret and in smallness.

Leadership Characteristic #5: Leaders Have an Eternal Perspective

Leaders must have an eternal perspective to maintain their diligence and pure motives. Our greatest promotion and reward in leadership will be in the age to come when the Lord, who sees all that we have put our hand to in this age, will fully reward us. Jesus called us to become great in His sight and in the age to come (Mt. 5:19; 18:4; 20:25-26; 23:11; Mk. 10:42-43; Lk. 6:23, 35; 9:48; 22:26). Jesus promised us riches, or treasure, in heaven (Mt. 6:20; 19:21; Mk. 10:21; Lk. 12:21, 33; 16:11; 18:22; Rev. 2:9; 3:18).

There is a direct and dynamic continuity between what we do now and what our position will be in the millennial kingdom when Jesus comes to rule on the earth. We need to be diligent in the day of smallness, knowing that God is watching and will reward us fully in the millennial kingdom. Jesus promises to cause the faithful to rule over many things in the age to come (Mt. 25:21; 23); to have authority over cities (Lk. 19:17, 19); to have power over nations (Rev. 2:26-27; Mt. 19:28; 20:21-23; Lk. 22:29-30). Jesus promised that we would sit on His throne with Him (Rev. 3:21) and that we would receive eternal rewards (Mt. 5:12; 6:4, 6, 18; 10:41-42; 16:27; Mk. 9:41; Lk. 6:23, 35; Rev. 22:12) and crowns in the age to come (Rev. 2:10; 3:11).

Leadership Characteristic #6: Leaders Persevere in Difficulty

This is a characteristic that marks a true leader. As we see that God values faithfulness in difficulty and smallness, then we are enabled to persevere through the difficult seasons that occur in the life of every leader. Many would-be leaders quit when they face difficulty or mistreatment, or when they are passed by and others are promoted before them. Persevering through these seasons with a diligent heart is what separates true leaders from non-leaders. Leadership is not a 100-yard dash, but a marathon. True leaders will stay steady for decades as they work towards accomplishing their God-given assignment without losing focus or drawing back.

All leaders will go through what I call the four seasons of life: the springtime of planting new things, the summertime when things grow, the autumn of the harvest, and the difficulty of winter when things die. Every leader goes through all four seasons. We must understand that persevering through the winter seasons is as critical to our ministry and personal development as the other three seasons of planting, growing, and harvesting.

Leadership Characteristic #7: Leaders Do what Needs to Be Done

An important aspect of leadership that is easily overlooked is that leaders do tasks that need to be done. Instead of only looking to start something new, or waiting for an exciting opportunity, leaders give themselves to tasks that need to be done right now. We see this is in the life of Joseph. We all know the story of how Joseph, as a teenage boy, was taken into slavery in Egypt and how Potiphar purchased him as a slave. While Joseph was merely a slave, he was promoted to the top position in Potiphar's house because of God's favor on his life and also because of his diligence to do simple tasks that needed to be done. It was not Joseph's vision to be the leader of Potiphar's house, but because Joseph was diligent to do the practical work that needed to be done, he was promoted.

Even after being thrown into prison unjustly, Joseph was diligent to do things that needed to be done inside the prison. No one in the prison demanded that Joseph make the prison a better place. However, Joseph took initiative to do what needed to be done and he was eventually promoted as the overseer of the entire prison. As Joseph's story shows us, leaders can make themselves indispensable simply by serving with diligence and a happy spirit.

Leadership Characteristic #8: Leaders Have a Teachable Spirit

Many are willing to serve as long as they do it on their own terms. However, the mark of a good leader is humility, with a teachable spirit. In other words, they are eager to learn from anyone and everyone, even from those under them who are less gifted, or from those who criticize them. A person with a humble spirit receives correction quickly and is easy to correct instead of being defensive and resistant to others who tell them how to do things differently. Proverbs tells us, "Whoever loves instruction loves knowledge and he who hates correction is stupid" (Prov. 12:1). A humble person will receive correction even from someone with a wrong spirit without being offended. I encourage people to view criticism as their "free research team." Disregarding correction is throwing away free advice and insight simply because you do not like the manner in which it comes.

The more you are promoted in leadership and the larger your platform becomes—whether in ministry, the marketplace, or in school—the more criticism you can expect to receive.

Leadership Characteristic #9: Leaders Serve for the Good of Others

As we grow in humility, we are more sensitive to serve for the good of others. Leaders are to be team players, honoring and receiving from others on their team, even those who are less gifted. They serve for the success of the people they minister to, rather than seeing them as stepping-stones to future success. Good leaders are focused on serving others in their calling and helping others to succeed, regardless of whether it entails them leaving to join another ministry. We must help them get to the next place in the will of God, even if it is another church or ministry.

We should view our ministry as a way to contribute to the success of others as we cheer them on to go higher and farther than we have. A good leader does not have the mentality of "owning" the people under him. We are to strengthen others first in their connection to Jesus and His will for their life, rather than their connection to us and our ministry. As it says in Proverbs, "He who earnestly seeks good finds favor" (Prov. 11:27). True leaders seek the good of those under them, even if it means helping them to join another ministry.

Leadership Characteristic #10: Leaders Take Fewer Privileges

A key principle of leadership found in the New Testament is that leaders who have more authority must take fewer privileges. As Paul states, "God has appointed these in the church: *first apostles* . . ." (1 Cor. 12:28). In other words, apostles were first in authority in the church. However, earlier in the same letter to the

Corinthians, Paul described apostles as *last,* as men condemned to death, who were hungry, thirsty and poorly clothed, beaten, homeless, reviled, and persecuted (1 Cor. 4:9-12). So although the apostles are first in authority, they are last in privilege.

The New Testament leadership model encourages those with more spiritual authority to take less privilege within their spiritual family. They should be willing to bear the most criticism, work the hardest, give the most money, and bear more difficulty than those who are under them. The larger our ministry becomes, the less privilege we should expect. Some in leadership today take more money and demand more honor as they increase in authority and their ministry grows in number. However, the New Testament principle is to take less privilege as our authority increases. All leaders will be tested in this.

Leadership Characteristic #11: Refusing to Have a Control Spirit

Good leaders must refuse to operate with a control spirit, meaning that they must not be possessive of the people in their ministry. The enemy tempts leaders to take an illegal control or ownership over the people who are part of their ministry. We naturally seek to protect our honor, money, and influence to make decisions that give us an advantage over others. However, when we operate in a spirit of self-interest, it creates anxiety in us and becomes divisive to others. Unity occurs when we approach relationships with a free spirit that asks for God's will, regardless of where it may lead the people under us. A control spirit in leadership is destructive to everyone involved, including the leader with a wrong spirit. Our highest goal in leadership should not be to gain more money and honor, but to obey the will of the Father and to help others do the same.

Leadership Characteristic #12: Being a Leader after God's Heart

Jeremiah prophesied that God would release shepherds with a heart after God in the end times, who would feed His people with knowledge of God's heart and ways (Jer. 3:15). These shepherds will walk out the first commandment by pursuing God's heart with all of theirs. By encountering God they will be equipped to feed others on the knowledge of who God is and what He is like. Those who accept the challenge of the Sacred Charge are answering the call to be forerunners who live after God's heart, even as David did (1 Sam. 13:14).

Ask yourself if you are exemplifying the kind of leadership that you would follow. Do you have a clear mission that you will greatly sacrifice for? Is your vision clear for others to understand and are you committed enough that they will follow you? When others grasp your vision and see you diligently working longer hours than they are, they will join you. People follow character more than credentials. It is not our title, credentials, or ministry numbers that foretell effective leadership. It is the way we carry our hearts and the way we express faithful devotion to Jesus and to the plans of His heart.

In this hour, the earth is looking for leaders to follow, and the Lord is calling for forerunners who will lead and take on the challenge of preparing others for ministry and Jesus' return. Whether our leadership placement is small or large, difficult or smooth, let us become diligent in all that we do.

CHAPTER 9

Speak Boldly

Being a Faithful Witness of the Truth

We are to boldly speak out as a faithful witness of the truth, with a fierce allegiance to Jesus and His Word. Of the seven commitments of the Sacred Charge, the call to *speak boldly as a faithful witness of the truth* is perhaps the most challenging and costly because it takes us out of the comfort zone, beyond our undisturbed private lives, into conflict and controversy. Thus, it will affect many of our relationships, our ministry reputation and even our finances. All who boldly speak the *full counsel* of God's Word will eventually face resistance and much rejection. This can be very painful.

Brother Yun, a leader in the Chinese underground church, was imprisoned and brutally persecuted for his faith in Jesus. When he visited our community at the International House of Prayer, in Kansas City, he told us something that astonished us. He said that the criticism and rejection that he received from other believers for standing for the truth was more painful than the torture he experienced in China as a prisoner for his faith. He told us that the pain he experienced from his physical beatings in prison was not as painful as the criticism that he received from the brethren.

The call to speak boldly is one that should not be taken lightly or flippantly. This commitment should be considered soberly and thoughtfully, as it will be costly to the messenger who chooses this narrow and difficult way. However, we all agree that the joy of pleasing God is well worth any cost to ourselves.

Jesus, the Faithful Witness

Jesus gave us insight into what it means to be a faithful witness. Throughout the gospel of John, Jesus is described as the One who fully embodies the truth of God. Jesus describes Himself as the way, *the truth*, and the life (Jn. 14:6). He reveals that His very purpose for coming into the world was to "bear witness to the truth" (Jn. 18:37). In fact, the first title ascribed to Jesus in the book of Revelation is "the faithful witness" (Rev. 1:5).

Jesus was not only a faithful witness in His earthly ministry. Even now, at the right hand of God, He remains the faithful witness. He will return once again to earth as the faithful witness, when He pours out His end-time glory and judgments. Jesus is the faithful witness now and for all eternity. The call to remain faithful in declaring both negative truths and positive promises is foundational to our role as a messenger of the truth.

We must be obedient to speak the *full counsel of God*, including both the positive and negative aspects of the truth (Acts 20:27). The Lord is calling His people to be faithful witnesses who boldly proclaim His truths now, and who also prepare themselves to speak of the unique dynamics that will occur in the generation in which the Lord returns.

Jesus always and only speaks the truth. During His earthly ministry, He did not back down in fear when the truth was difficult for people to receive. He did not avoid speaking truths that were negative, nor did He exaggerate the positive things with flattery. His words were filled with truth. Jesus did not dilute the truth when it came as a rebuke or a warning of judgment. Speaking the truth is one vital aspect of how God expresses His love for us. How would you feel about your physician if he withheld the truth from you about a life-threatening disease that could be cured if responded to in a timely way? We would charge any doctor of malpractice who withheld the truth from his patient because he wanted to stay positive and appear loving. In a similar way, God raises messengers who will faithfully tell the negative aspects of the truth while there is still time to respond and receive God's mercy and healing. Jesus is a powerful and loving Bridegroom King who desires that we give Him all of our heart as He manifests His power. He is also a righteous Judge who will remove all that hinders love. He wants love to fill the earth.

Because Jesus experienced resistance and rejection when declaring difficult truths, He understands the pressures we face in doing the same. It was not His miracles or His works of justice towards the poor that led to His death, but His refusal to dilute the truth about the spiritual condition of the people of that day, and about Himself. It was His role as a faithful witness that was the catalyst for His murder.

The Call to Be a Faithful Witness of the Truth

A faithful witness must be a *firsthand witness* of what the Word and the Spirit are saying. Being a faithful witness implies that we speak out of what we have seen in our personal encounters with Jesus and His Word. We can only do this as we receive firsthand revelation of the truth, rather than merely repeating what others say. Standing firm in proclaiming the truth requires that we cultivate depth in the Word. It will not be enough to just know a Bible verse or echo what we have heard others proclaim.

To be faithful implies that we speak without drawing back in fear or intimidation. Ezekiel the prophet was exhorted by the Lord to not be "dismayed" by the negative response to his message, but to be faithful in proclaiming the words that the Lord had given to him (Ezek. 2:6-7; 3:9-11). Jeremiah was also commanded not to be dismayed by the faces of those he was sent to, but to stand as a "fortified city" and an "iron pillar" against much resistance in his day (Jer. 1:17-18). We must not back down from speaking the truth that exposes the false teachings that are spreading rapidly in this hour. Our witness for truth must be *biblical, clear, bold, tender,* and *humble.*

To be *biblical* means that we must stay within the boundary lines of Scripture in all that we say. Some "teachers" have good intentions when they say things that undermine the truths set forth in the Scriptures. Some will speak anything that they see in vision or a prophetic dream without regard for whether it honors the Scriptures. All subjective prophetic revelation must honor the truths that are in the written Word of God.

To be *clear* means we must speak truth in a straightforward way that is easily understood by our hearers. We are not to obscure or dull the cutting edge of truth by lessening it because of having a man-pleasing spirit.

To be *bold* means we must not be intimidated by the fear of rejection when speaking truth. We speak boldly because we understand that only by receiving God's truth can people hope to experience more of His love and mercy.

To be *tender* means we speak truth without bitterness or anger as we seek the benefit of our hearers. The point of speaking boldly is not to win an argument, or to prove that we are right, or to get even. We speak it for the benefit of the hearer so that they have a chance to respond and receive more of God's love and power.

To be *humble* means we speak the truth without a personal agenda. Do not let the pendulum swing to the other side by falling into the trap of speaking the truth to prove how courageous and bold you are. Some build their ministries and establish their ministry identity around criticizing and exposing others. The point of speaking boldly is not to gain a following as being the only ones who are courageous enough to tell the whole truth, but to help people connect more with Jesus.

A Sevenfold Expression of Speaking Boldly as a Faithful Witness

As we approach the end of the age, the "gospel of the kingdom will be preached in all the whole world as a witness to *all the nations*" (Mt. 24:24). There will be a complete witness of the *full* message, or the *full truth,* of the kingdom in every nation. The full message is that Jesus our king is coming back to take over all the nations. This witness of the gospel includes much more than the message of forgiveness that introduces it. I rejoice in the message of forgiveness because I need it so much. However, the gospel of the kingdom is not limited to the glorious message of forgiveness so that we escape hell. It is a call to be deeply involved with our King and His kingdom forever.

There are seven purposes that are accomplished when God's people give a faithful witness to the full truth of the kingdom.

Speak Boldly: Personal Salvation

The first thing that is accomplished by giving a faithful witness of the truth is that people receive *personal salvation*. This is so glorious. The angels have joy when sinners repent (Lk. 15:10). In the generation in which the Lord returns, a great harvest of souls will come into the kingdom from all nations. John saw "*a great multitude which no one could number*, of all nations, tribes, people, and tongues, standing before the throne" (Rev. 7:9). When John asked where this great multitude came from, he was told, "These are the ones who come out of the *great tribulation*" (Rev. 7:14). This glorious message of forgiveness is the starting point in our relationship with Jesus, the King of kings, and of our involvement in His kingdom forever.

Speak Boldly: Exposing Lies

A second purpose of giving a faithful witness to the truth is that it *exposes lies* that deceive and seduce people into error. Jesus teaches us that "many" will respond to false teachers and prophets in the end times (Mt. 24:5, 11). We are responsible to expose the harmful lies of false prophets and teachers. Jesus commended the church in Ephesus for having "tested those who say they are apostles and are not, and have found them liars" (Rev. 2:2). They evaluated those who claimed to be apostles and, finding that they did not bear the fruit of true apostles, they exposed them as false.

The Scriptures are clear that we must tell the truth so as to expose lies that perpetuate *destructive* doctrines and behavior (Mt. 18:5-7; 1 Cor. 5:1-11; 2 Cor. 11:12-15; 1 Thes. 5:14, 21; 2 Thes. 3:6-15; Rev. 2:2, 14-15, 20). It is essential that we do this in the *right process and with a right spirit*, in tenderness instead of pride. While being committed to exposing *destructive* doctrines and behavior of a few, we are also committed to cultivating a culture of honor that blesses the vast majority of other ministries. We bless their budding virtues that have not yet matured, regardless of their ministry deficiencies. In other words, we only expose *destructive* doctrines and behavior, not the weaknesses and deficiencies in other ministries or people.

I distinguish between heresies, deceptions, and errors. *Heresies* are teachings that keep someone from receiving salvation. They are significant lies about Jesus and the way of salvation. *Deceptions* are teachings that hinder believers from fellowshipping with others in the larger Body of Christ because they hold people in bondage to wrong ideas. We expose heresies and deceptions. *Errors* are wrong beliefs in the secondary issues of the kingdom. They come up short of the full understanding of God's Word. Every one has some errors. I have never met a person who has perfect understanding of God's Word. We extend much grace with patience to one another's errors in the secondary issues of the kingdom.

Speak Boldly: Prophetic Invitations and Warnings

The third way we may give a faithful witness to the truth is by proclaiming God's *invitations and warnings* concerning the things that are yet to come. "The Lord God does nothing, unless He reveals His secret to His . . . prophets" (Amos 3:7). The greatest revival and the most severe pressures in all history will occur in the final decades just before Jesus returns. We announce that the greatest revival in history is sure to come. All are invited to participate in it by becoming vessels who make known the love and power of Jesus to others. Many will reject this gracious invitation from God. If they persist in rebellion against Him, then we must warn them of the coming judgment, that they may repent and receive the mercy of God.

For the sake of love, Jesus wants the nations to hear about the positive and negative things that are coming *before* they come, to give them opportunity to respond. Jesus wants the nations to understand the revival that is sure to come to the Church and the judgments that are sure to come upon the Antichrist's empire.

Because God is just, He insists that the rebellious be warned *before* the judgment occurs. The Lord told the prophet Ezekiel of his responsibility to make known to his generation the truth about the judgments of God that were coming in his day (Ezek. 33:3-8). The Lord showed Ezekiel that if he were faithful to proclaim the coming judgments, the rebellious would have sufficient opportunity to repent and receive God's mercy. If they refused God's mercy, they themselves would be responsible for the judgment that came upon them. However, if Ezekiel did not faithfully warn them of the coming judgment, then he would be partially responsible for their blood. This would apply even to the reprobate. There are people who are permanently hardened in their hatred of God so that they have no desire to ever repent.

Speak Boldly: Understanding God's Judgments

The fourth sense in which faithful witnesses proclaim the full truth of the kingdom is by bringing understanding about God's judgments. It is not enough to make known the *fact* that God's judgments are coming—we must give the *reason* for them. We are to give the *why* behind the *what*. Forerunner messengers are to help the people make sense of God's judgments so that they do not fall into the common confusion that God's judgments contradict His love. In fact, God's judgments come to remove all that hinders love. In other words, His judgments are *expressions of His love*. Many who misunderstand God's judgments are offended and angry with God because of them. The faithful witness of the truth in all nations will help multitudes receive the love of God in the midst of the coming judgments rather than be offended at Jesus and refuse His love. The essence of judgment is God intervening to deliver the oppressed and to stop the oppressors. Think of the implications of a God who did not intervene to stop the oppressors. What would you think of a father who claimed to love his children but did not intervene to stop a perverse man from abusing them? It would be difficult to believe that such a father loved his children.

God's judgments are released to deliver His children from wicked oppressors. This is an expression of His love for His children. In the midst of those very judgments, God offers mercy to the oppressors, if they will only repent and receive it. Isaiah proclaimed that when God's judgments are in the earth, the inhabitants of the world learn righteousness (Isa. 26:9). God's judgments against the wicked are not the same as His discipline against the Church. Many fail to distinguish between His loving discipline to remove compromise from His people with His angry judgments against those who continually oppress His people.

It is essential that a faithful witness of the truth be given in this vital area so that believers will grow in love for Jesus instead of being offended at His leadership in the midst of judgment. We must rightly interpret His judgments in order to trust His leadership so that we may mature in love for Him.

Jeremiah prophesied that in the last days God would give His people a supernatural ability to perceive His loving purposes in sending His judgments. He prophesied, "In the latter days you will *understand it perfectly*" (Jer. 23:20). Jeremiah went on to prophesy that God's messengers would *consider*, or search out, the Word of God to gain understanding of God's heart behind His end-time judgments (Jer. 30:24). Daniel also explains this same reality by saying that "those of the *people who understand* shall instruct many" (Dan. 11:33).

Many misunderstand the central point of Jesus' return and why He is releasing His judgments. The Lord will correct this misunderstanding by raising up those who will give a faithful witness to the truth. The return of Jesus as Bridegroom, King, and Judge is called "the blessed hope" (Titus 2:13). Jesus' end-time plan to prepare the Church and the earth for His return is part of this glorious hope. It includes the greatest outpouring of the Spirit and the most intense outpouring of judgment in all history. The very heart of the end-time message is that Jesus will come in person to rule all the nations and that His judgments will remove all oppression and rebellion against God from the planet. This will result in all nations living in the joy of God's manifest presence with unprecedented prosperity, righteousness, unity, and goodness. The devil will be thrown into prison and all evil laws and leaders will be replaced by those that are righteous and good (Rev. 20:1-6).

Speak Boldly: Eschatological Intercession

Fifthly, one of the significant by products of the full truth of the kingdom being preached in every nation is that anointed intercessors will be in place in every nation.

I use the term *eschatological intercession* to refer to inter-cession that is focused on the unique events of the generation in which the Lord returns. (*Eschatology* means the study of the end times). Only one generation in history will witness Jesus' return to earth. Intercessors living in that generation will actually ask Him to come back to earth and take over the leadership of their nation. The Spirit and the Bride will say, "Come, Lord Jesus!" (Rev. 22:17, 20). This cry is more than a cry for revival. It is an intercessory invitation for King Jesus to take over their nation. It is more than a personal cry of devotion; it is a covenantal, politi-cal cry that will beckon Jesus to come and take over the govern-ment of their nation as King of kings. Every nation on earth will experience a revival in the end times. Thus, Jesus will have a people who intercede for His leadership to replace the ungodly leaders in their nation (Rev. 11:15).

Through prayer and obedience, we specifically open the door to invite Jesus to reign in each area of our life, including our heart, family, finances, circumstances, and even our nation. The psalmist taught that the heavens belong to the Lord, "but the earth He has given to the children of men" (Ps. 115:16). In other words, God has entrusted the realm of the earth to humans. Therefore, He waits for His people to invite His leadership over the earth through their intercession. God honors the authority He has given to human beings. Each person has a particular sphere of influence where they have authority to invite the Lord's leadership.

God gave the governmental decision-making authority of the earth to humans. Just as Jesus spoke to Jerusalem, "You shall see Me no more till you say 'Blessed is He who comes in the name of the Lord'" (Mt. 23:39), Jesus will not impose His kingship on any nation. He comes only after He is *invited to come* to that nation by His covenant people in that nation. From every nation of the earth, Jesus will receive this covenant invitation, beckoning and welcoming His return.

Speak Boldly: Judicial Hardening

When faithful witnesses proclaim the truth in power about Jesus' lordship and second coming to all nations, there is yet a sixth purpose that is accomplished—it brings the hidden hardness of man's heart to the surface. This spiritual dynamic is sometimes referred to as the *"judicial hardening"* of the heart. It is a theological concept that describes the final hardening process of a person's heart against God. In Moses' day, Pharaoh was an example of judicial hardening. Even though he experienced Moses' miracles and prophecies, Pharaoh's heart did not turn to God. On the contrary, he continually hardened his heart more and more against the Lord, which ultimately led to God hardening his heart (Ex. 4:21; 8:15, 32; 9:12, 34; 10:1, 20, 27; 11:10; 14:3, 8, 17).

The purpose of the judicial hardening of the heart is for the deep, hidden hatred of God that works in the hearts of some wicked men to be brought to the surface. Then it will no longer be hidden behind politically correct façades; these people with permanently hardened hearts will create a hostile environment in which the power of God is displayed with great might. Paul explains that God hardened Pharaoh in order to display His power through him to all the earth. "For the Scripture says to Pharaoh, 'For this very purpose I have raised you up, that I may show My power in you, and that My name may be declared in all the earth'" (Rom. 9:17). The combination of anointed prophetic preaching that is confirmed with miracles can act as an accelerant, bringing the rebellion that is already in man's heart to the surface.

Paul speaks of this reality occurring in the end times, and prophesies that *God will send* a strong delusion that the reprobate should believe a lie (2 Thes. 2:11-12). God's justice is openly displayed as He allows what is *hidden* in the hearts of the reprobate to be openly manifest for all to see. In this way, God's justice is seen in removing these evil men from the earth through His end-time judgments. Only after the fullness of men's hatred of God comes to the surface in actions will God release the fullness of His wrath against them. It is not enough for them to hate God; they must walk it out in actions before God's justice is clearly displayed in His judgments against them.

Many wicked people will not receive the invitation of God's love and mercy that will be given to them in the end times. They will choose to worship the Antichrist (Rev. 13:8). God will still require faithful witnesses who must speak the truth boldly to the wicked, for in this way Jesus' perfect love and justice will be manifest in all that He does. He will offer His love to His enemies and will show His justice by giving them opportunity to receive it and by clearly warning them of the consequences of rejecting it (Rev. 14:6-11). Jesus will even take the very evil deeds that these hardened people commit against the saints and use them for His glory. He will overrule their plans for evil and cause them to bring about the good of His people (Gen. 50:20; Rom. 8:28; 9:17-22).

God's justice demands that wicked men be given a fair warning of judgment, even if they refuse His warning. He always warns the wicked before they receive the judgments they deserve. God is just and true in all that He does, even in the administration of His end-time judgments. Thus, the saints will declare, "Just and true are Your ways," when they witness God's end-time judgments (Rev. 15:2-4; 19:2).

Speak Boldly: Praying for Judgment against the Antichrist

There is a seventh purpose of giving a faithful witness of the truth that will only occur in the final three and a half years of this age. Faithful witnesses will proclaim the necessity of interceding for judgment against the Antichrist's reprobate empire. Reprobate people will be so hardened in their hatred of God that they have no desire to ever repent. As Moses prayed for God to release His judgments against a reprobate Pharaoh (Ex. 7-12), so the saints will pray for God to release judgment against the Antichrist's empire, which seeks to oppress and kill the saints.

The saints will also pray and ask God to replace the Antichrist's evil governmental leaders with His own godly leadership.

In that day, the prayers of *all* the saints from throughout history will be released against the Antichrist's empire (Rev. 8:3-5; Ps. 149:6-9). The Holy Spirit is not calling people to pray for judgment now, but He will do so in the final three and a half years of this age. Right now, we *always pray for mercy to stop God's judgment against a nation*. The only exception to this will be during the final three and a half years of this age.

Conclusion

The call to speak boldly as a faithful witness of the truth is an important part of God's end-time purpose. It is part of the declaration of the full gospel of the kingdom that serves as the catalyst to His return. Therefore, let us follow the Lamb, the ultimate faithful witness, that we also might "bear witness to the truth" (Jn. 18:37).

NEW!

MIKEBICKLE.org

FREE Resource Library

This library comprises a wealth of resources from over 25 years of Mike's teaching ministry and provides access to hundreds of resources in various formats, including streaming video, downloadable video, and audio, accompanied by study notes and transcriptions—absolutely free of charge. Here you will find some of Mike's most beloved titles, including *The Life of David, The Song of Songs, The First Commandment, The Book of Romans, The Book of Revelation,* and much more. Mike has always encouraged people to freely copy and share his teachings, so we encourage you to take full advantage of these resources and share them widely with your friends and family: *"Our copyright is the right to copy."* New content is continually being prepared and expanded from Mike's archives, and all new teachings will be added immediately.

Subscribe to Mike Bickle's FREE video podcast.

internships
Encounter God. Do His Works. Change the World.

Each of our four internships are committed to praying for the release of the fullness of God's power and purpose as interns actively win the lost, heal the sick, feed the poor, and minister in the power of the Holy Spirit. Our vision is to work in relationship with the larger Body of Christ to serve the Great Commission, as we seek to walk out the two great commandments to love God and people. Our desire is to see each intern build strong relationships and lifelong friendships.

INTRO TO IHOP-KC

A 3-month program for those joining IHOP–KC staff. This program offers classes about IHOP–KC's values, ministries, and structure, and gives practical skills for you to succeed long-term as an intercessory missionary. This program is designed for both families and singles.

ONE THING

A 6-month program for single young adults.

SIMEON COMPANY

A 3-month program for those 50 years and over, whether married or single.

FIRE IN THE NIGHT

A 3-month program for young adults between the ages of 18–30 who cry out to the Lord between the hours of midnight and 6:00am.

International House of Prayer University
3535 E. Red Bridge Road, Kansas City, MO 64137
816.763.0200 • internships@ihop.org • IHOP.org/internships

INTERNATIONAL HOUSE OF PRAYER

MISSIONS BASE OF KANSAS CITY

Combining 24/7 Prayers for Justice
with 24/7 Works of Justice

Since September 19, 1999, we have continued in night and day prayer with worship as the foundation of our ministry to win the lost, heal the sick, and make disciples as we labor alongside the larger Body of Christ to serve the Great Commission and to live as forerunners who prepare the way for the return of Jesus. By the grace of God, we are committed to combining 24/7 prayers for justice with 24/7 works for justice until the Lord returns. We are best equipped to reach out to others when our lives are rooted in prayer that focuses on intimacy with God and intercession for a breakthrough of the fullness of God's power and purpose for this generation.

For more information on our internships, conferences, university, live prayer room webcast, and more, please visit our website at IHOP.org.

International House of Prayer Missions Base
3535 E. Red Bridge Road, Kansas City, MO 64137
816.763.0200 • info@ihop.org • IHOP.org

IHOPU
INTERNATIONAL HOUSE OF PRAYER UNIVERSITY

Encounter God. Do His Works. Change the World.

Forerunner School of Ministry
Forerunner Music Academy
Forerunner Media Institute
eSchool & Distance Learning

IHOPU's mandate is to equip and send out believers who love Jesus and others wholeheartedly, to preach the Word, heal the sick, serve the poor, plant churches and start houses of prayer, and proclaim the return of Jesus.

IHOPU stands in an environment of 24/7 prayer with worship and a thriving missions base. We are establishing a community built around the centrality of Scripture, prayer, and worship in a context where the Word of God is continuously expressed through teaching, singing, praying, and ministry to one another.

International House of Prayer University
3535 E. Red Bridge Road, Kansas City, MO 64137
816.763.0243 • ihopu@ihop.org • IHOP.org/university